PRAISE FOR *WHY ARE THERE SNOWBLOWERS IN MIAMI?*

"Straight-forward and transformative at the same time, Goldstein's book offers brilliant new strategies to resolve even the most entrenched and complex problems. Following his wise advice will enable your workforce to be able to focus more closely on the business at hand—resulting in a nimble, forward-thinking, and successful organization!"

—Marshall Goldsmith, winner of Thinkers50 Leadership Award 2015 and *New York Times* best-selling author of *What Got You Here Won't Get You There* and *Triggers*

"We live in an increasingly complex and changing world; yesterday's formulas for attaining success simply no longer apply. Steve Goldstein's Five Principles take us out of our comfortable routines—providing us with the courage to act anew and a straight-forward wisdom that will lead to meaningful rewards."

—Peter Georgescu, Chairman Emeritus, Young & Rubicam

"Steve is one of those leaders who can operate equally well in large and small companies, from American Express to Silicon Valley start-ups. Not only is he equally adept at operating up and down the scale of businesses, he's also great at both strategy AND implementation, a very rare combination. This book is the distillation of a long, successful business career and is a must-read for any leader who understands that engagement is essential for successful results. Every leader will find that Steve's Five Principles of Engagement break it down in a way that they can easily see what they need to do."

—Allen Morgan, director of Idealab; former partner, Mayfield Fund; former partner, Wilson Sonsini; start-up Sherpa

"*Why Are There Snowblowers in Miami?* offers a treasure trove of leadership insight. Discover why you should question everything, break the meeting habit, and recognize that the best suggestions often don't come from inside the C-Suite but from the window washers on the other side of the glass. Steve Goldstein is a natural storyteller with a lifetime of experience and wisdom to boot."

—Ron Friedman, PhD, author *of The Best Place to Work: The Art and Science of Creating an Extraordinary Workplace*

"I loved *Why Are There Snowblowers in Miami?* from the first time I heard about it, especially since I often encounter dysfunctional companies. Steve's vast corporate and entrepreneurial experience serves the reader well by avoiding consultant jargon, buzzwords, and complex theories and instead offers a straightforward, accessible, and hands-on approach to managing people, customers, and business operations that everyone in business can relate to and learn from. His often amusing and always instructive stories are a bonus! Enjoy!"

—David Nour, growth strategist and best-selling author of *Relationship Economics*

"Having known and worked with Steve for more than twenty-five years, I have seen first-hand the powerful effects from applying the principles laid out in this book. Steve is a wonderful storyteller with a gift for engagement with others and the challenges at hand. And, his stories are the best possible kind: funny and wise."

—Douglas K. Smith, author of *The Wisdom of Teams*

"Steve's book pulls you in right from the very beginning with a hilarious (but unfortunately not uncommon) story of corporate dysfunction. He then goes on to describe and illustrate Five Principles of Engagement that will guide executives, middle managers, and leaders of all stripes in successfully running their organization. Through engagement with their employees, customers, and even themselves, leaders will find a goldmine of insightful and practical advice in this book."

—James M. Kerr, management consultant, *INC* columnist, and author of *The Executive Checklist: A Guide to Setting Direction and Managing Change*

WHY ARE THERE SNOWBLOWERS IN MIAMI?

TRANSFORM YOUR BUSINESS USING THE FIVE PRINCIPLES OF ENGAGEMENT

STEVEN D. GOLDSTEIN

GREENLEAF
BOOK GROUP PRESS

Published by Greenleaf Book Group Press
Austin, Texas
www.gbgpress.com

Distributed by Greenleaf Book Group

For ordering information or special discounts for bulk purchases, please contact Greenleaf Book Group at PO Box 91869, Austin, TX 78709, 512.891.6100.

Design and composition by Greenleaf Book Group and Sheila Parr
Cover design by Greenleaf Book Group and Sheila Parr

Cataloging-in-Publication data is available.

Print ISBN: 978-1-62634-323-8

eBook ISBN: 978-1-62634-324-5

Part of the Tree Neutral® program, which offsets the number of trees consumed in the production and printing of this book by taking proactive steps, such as planting trees in direct proportion to the number of trees used: www.treeneutral.com

TreeNeutral

Printed in the United States of America on acid-free paper

16 17 18 19 20 21   10 9 8 7 6 5 4 3 2 1

First Edition

To my wife Varda, who has been my partner and wingman every step of the way on this journey, and to Lauren and Billy who make me so proud. Thank you.

CONTENTS

ACKNOWLEDGMENTS

For a number of years, I felt there was a book inside me, perhaps way deep down. As with many things, the hardest part is getting started. To those of you who encouraged, cajoled, and pushed me to go forward with this project, I am truly grateful and appreciative of your confidence in me.

I will also be eternally grateful to the first boss I had after I received my MBA degree, Hank Walsh at Burroughs Corp., who showed me that you should behave exactly the same way whether you are with the chairman of the board or the janitor. It was an invaluable lesson.

I would like to thank all the leaders I interviewed for this book: Craig Dinsell, Andy Florance, Don Gogel, Tom Hale, Claes Landberg, Rick McVey, Denis Picard, John Wilton, and Eli Zabar; their stories and experiences truly demonstrate the range and scope of engagement in action.

Finally, I would like to thank Jeanne Martinet, who helped me write this book. I could not have done it without her.

INTRODUCTION

They say the definition of insanity is doing the same thing over and over and expecting a different result. But what if you don't even *notice* the result?

From 1996 to 1998, I was president of the credit card business for Sears, which at the time was the largest retail credit card in the United States. The company was headquartered in Chicago, but I spent much of my time traveling around the country visiting our many operating centers. Occasionally I would give speeches at industry gatherings. One very cold January, I was lucky enough to be speaking at a conference in Miami—which at 85 degrees was definitely more comfortable than the 10-degree temperature back in Chicago. In fact, a major blizzard was starting to blast the Midwest.

Because Sears Credit was used for more than half the purchases made in the stores, I always made a point to visit the local Sears store wherever I happened to be. I used these visits to speak with salespeople on the floor—to understand what was going on in the business and with our customers and to find out what my group could be doing better to support them and build sales.

When I entered the store in Miami I found myself in the Garden Center, where there was an attractive array of lawn mowers, shovels, rakes, hedge trimmers, and barbecue grills—everything you needed to take care of your yard. It looked like a well-stocked department, everything in its proper place. And then suddenly I saw them, right next to the mowers. Four *snowblowers*. What? In Miami? I blinked and looked more closely, thinking maybe I was seeing something else, something that only *resembled* snowblowers. But no, that's what they were.

Perplexed, I went to track down a salesperson. I found a man nicely dressed in khaki pants and a plaid sport coat named Peter who looked close to retirement age. After introducing myself, I asked him, "Can you tell me why you have snowblowers on the floor?"

Without missing a beat he replied, "The snowblowers? Oh, they send them to us every year. Eventually we send them back in April because of course there's no snow here." I asked how long this had been going on, and he said, "For as long as I can remember." As I chatted more with Peter, he went on to tell me that his manager, along with his manager's boss, called corporate every year to ask why they kept sending them. The answer they got was always the same: "It's part of the nationwide allocation."

"Do you ever sell any of them?" I asked him, curious.

"Actually, we did sell one last year," Peter replied with a big smile, "to a couple who were buying it for their kids in Minnesota. They said they were going to take it with them in their minivan when they drove up to visit them for Christmas."

The following day, after a long delay in the airport and a very bumpy plane ride home, I was back in the Chicago office for our weekly leadership meeting. The biggest issue of this particular meeting was the massive snowstorm—its impact on our supply chain and what we needed to do to mitigate the myriad problems it might cause.

Almost the minute the meeting began, someone jumped in with, "We have a major out-of-stock problem with snow-blowers, in the areas affected by the blizzard."

"We do have them," another colleague said, "but they're stuck in a distribution center, which is unfortunately right in the middle of the storm, and it will probably take two to three days to move them out."

"Well, we have four in Miami," I said wryly.

Everyone in the room looked at me as if I were crazy, until I told them about my visit to the Miami store. There were a few jokes made about the absurdity of the situation. Then I asked the group in all seriousness if anyone knew what the explanation was for how and why these snow-blowers ended up in Miami.

"It's probably part of the historical allocation formulas, and we definitely need to take a look at that some time," was the response I got. Everyone seemed to be fine with that answer, and we moved on to several other issues before we adjourned. As I was walking back to my office after the meeting, I found myself thinking, But how did snowblow-ers get into the formula for Miami in the first place? And why doesn't anybody care?

Though it was a simple question, the answer is any-thing but simple. Did someone actually develop a plan that included sending snowblowers to a place where the only snow in recorded history was a few flakes on one day in 1977? Of course not. Somewhere along the line, a mistake was made—or a clumsy system instituted—that has since been buried in layers of operational morass. Needless to say, a few snowblowers sitting in a store in Florida does not constitute a major business disaster. But the image has stuck in my mind all these years because it has always seemed to me a perfect metaphor for what happens when there is a lack of engagement within a large organization.

Peter, his manager, and the department manager no longer paid any attention to the snowblowers, having become numb to the situation after repeated efforts to fix it came to nothing. The store manager, district manager, and regional vice president either didn't know there were snowblowers in Miami, or did know but chose not to do anything about it. Probably each of these people was thinking to himself: *How deep is this problem? Do I really want to go there? Whose toes will I be stepping on if I try to correct this?* The executives back at corporate headquarters had no idea and had other issues occupying their time. And even when I brought it up at the weekly leadership meeting, the allocation problem was brushed aside as being both too unimportant and too complicated to look into at that moment (or any other moment, for that matter.)

Almost all companies have their own version of this kind of seemingly inexplicable mix-up or missed opportunity, and the truth is that most of the time the companies are not even aware of it. No one knows why it happened or who is responsible for straightening it out. No one "owns it."

I decided to write this book because I have seen hundreds of examples of this kind of corporate dysfunction—ranging from minor to major—that I have found are usually the result of some kind of internal disengagement. Sometimes the consequences can be serious, leading to major performance problems. I've never been someone who looks the other way; in fact, I tend to be the one who asks, "Why do we do it this way?" "How can we do it better?" "Do we need to do it at all?" and other questions that get to the core of the matter.

I've spent the majority of my career untangling the spaghetti—identifying problems, and leading teams to solve these problems in order to increase productivity and profit. More important, I engage with employees to understand what they can do to help the company succeed—and what they can do to better serve customers. These employees derive great satisfaction from seeing their thoughts and ideas generating results. Their work becomes more interesting, they are more likely to keep their jobs and, even better, have a greater opportunity to move up in the organization. They realize that asking questions is a good thing as opposed to something to be afraid of. I love watching people move beyond their comfort zone and really excel at what they do.

From the diverse experiences I have had as a CEO of several global companies, as a consultant, as an advisor to private equity firms, as a board member, and as an investor, I've learned what works and what doesn't work; and I've developed a unique model based on what I have identified as the Five Principles of Engagement. Along with true stories from my own experiences and firsthand anecdotes and insights culled from interviews I have conducted with influential leaders—CEOs from both the corporate and nonprofit arenas—this book offers leaders practical techniques derived from these all-important Five Principles.

I am excited to be able to share with other leaders the knowledge, tools, and programs that I've developed and had so much success with over the years.

Engagement is where it starts.

CHAPTER ONE

FRESH EYES: HOW ENGAGEMENT BEGINS

"We can't solve problems by using the same kind of thinking we used when we created them."

—Albert Einstein

We all hear the same excuses every day. "That's just the way things work here." "Some day we'll have to look into that." "We're just too big to change quickly." But why does it take so long to accomplish things in large companies? Why aren't leaders more courageous, and why is just sitting back and waiting a common strategy? Why is no one demanding more of themselves and others? The answer to these questions is complicated, but I believe that a big part of it has to do with a lack of engagement—on one or on multiple levels.

Obviously, the term "engagement" can mean many different things. So what do I mean by engagement in the context of leadership and running a company? Engagement, in my experience, means adopting an active, roll-up-your-sleeves style that fundamentally takes an outside-in view of everything in the organization. It means being totally present; it means looking in places where it's easier *not* to look. It means being aware of what's really going on—not only looking but also *seeing*. An engaged leader is one who is interested in finding out what employees think about the business instead of solely relying on the management team and reports. An engaged leader interacts in an authentic way with customers to see what their buying experience is like and if they buy out of habit or out of conscious choice. An engaged leader has the confidence and courage to admit that everything is not working perfectly. Engagement also means being hyperinquisitive—asking questions, and then asking more questions. It means redefining how you see problems. It means being comfortable with constantly creating and leading change. It means communicating well and motivating everyone to win. It means acting like an owner in every sense of the word.

Several years ago, a consulting firm I was working with was hired to help a company that was experiencing performance problems in several areas. This company was in the business of providing customer contact services to companies that outsourced their sales, customer service, and other routine functions. At the time they hired us, they were at risk of losing clients faster than they could replace them.

My team and I met individually with each member of the management team and listened to their concerns, and to their ideas about what they were planning to do to address the problems—that is, *the problems as they had identified them*. Their assessment was completely insular. In many cases, they were oblivious to many of the important issues—not unlike Sears had been to the snowblowers in Miami situation. Predictably, their recommendations were that costs should be further reduced to make up for the shortfall in lost revenue. On the face of it, that's not an unreasonable course of action, in that it would help profitability in the short term. But it fails to attack the problems at their source.

I knew that we needed to get another perspective; we needed to see how the company's clients perceived the company and why those clients were jumping ship—because the leadership team either didn't know, or didn't want to tell us at that point. We spoke with several of these clients, who were more than willing to tell us why they were unhappy with both the service levels and lack of responsiveness in dealing with their problems, and who also informed us that they were actively considering choosing another provider as soon as their contracts expired.

Joe, one client I spoke to, was a vice president of a large wireless carrier. "We outsource a big portion of our customer service functions," he said, "so that we could have predictability about service levels and cost, and also to get critical information about what is on our customers' minds. The cost portion is fine, since we negotiated a fixed price contract, but everything else is not working as expected." When I asked Joe to be more specific, he said, "Service levels are below expectations, it takes too long to address problems, and I keep hearing about technology glitches to explain their service level problems—but isn't technology supposed to be what their business is all about?"

Joe had an excellent point. How does a company whose core business is servicing have technology "glitches" that are so bad they cause customers to leave? I knew we needed to see firsthand what was going on in these call centers, so we organized a field trip to visit one. When we arrived at this location, the management team—while very welcoming to us—appeared somewhat uneasy. They were obviously wondering exactly why we were there.

The call center was a cubicle-filled room about the size of a football field. As we entered, we were struck by the sight of old-fashioned computer monitors—the big beige ones that occupy most of a desk and had not been on the market for at least ten years—as well as desk chairs and desks that were missing an arm here, a leg there . . . I was stunned. Several people were actually wearing headsets with duct tape on them! After walking no more than twenty-five feet, I was barely able to speak; I was so shocked by the conditions.

We spent the better part of a day at the center. We stopped at individual workstations and watched and listened to how people did their jobs, and saw how difficult the company made it for them to be responsive to customers. It was as if they were running a race uphill wearing fifty-pound backpacks, while someone on top of the mountain was throwing rocks at them. It certainly was not a work environment that was conducive to being on the phone for eight hours per day and dealing with individual customer issues.

I sat next to an agent named Judy and put on a headset so that I could listen in on her calls. I immediately noticed that simple questions from a customer required complicated actions on her part. So, after a few calls, I asked her why her responses were so hard to formulate. Judy explained that the old computers and software applications they were using made things that should be easy much more difficult. "I have to look at one screen, write down the information on a post-it, then go to another screen to see something else, make a note of that, and then go to a third screen. After I figure it out, then I can give the customer an answer." When I asked her how she would change things, Judy immediately listed six things that would eliminate most of the problems. She had the solutions—but had never been asked for her opinion.

We organized some of the staff into discussion groups in a conference room. As I often do, I asked pretty basic questions to encourage people to open up, like "How's it going?" "What's it like to work here?" "What do you need to do your job better?" "What are your customers saying?" At the end of the day, we had pages of notes and a very good idea about (1) what was wrong; (2) how to fix it; (3) what the employees needed to do a better job; and (4) most important, why the employee turnover of this unit was almost 100 percent.

That night I had dinner with the CEO. He wanted to know how the field trip had gone. Because it was my understanding that he traveled extensively around the world to visit his company's call centers, I asked him what his impressions of this particular one were, and he said, "I don't think I've been to that one in quite some time." I told him who we had met with and what we had learned, and I gave him some initial ideas as to how to dramatically change the situation. It was not a question of fixing one or two simple issues; this was a systemic problem created over a period of years that required a total rethink of how the business was conducted. I suggested that he select a great young leader, put him or her in charge of this center, and provide the money to create a workplace and environment that would enable the new leader to hire, motivate, and retain great staff. I bet him that within twelve months, this center would outperform every other one in the system and that they could then use what they learned here to address their underlying business issues and apply those changes throughout their network.

Ultimately, while the company implemented a number of other recommendations we made, they decided they could not afford to implement the "new call center project" we outlined for them; they felt it was too much change to undergo. But the question is, could they really afford *not* to implement this? Things cannot change unless you confront the dysfunction at its source.

In most organizations the only people dealing with customers are at the lower levels, like Judy, the call center operator. These employees often feel disenfranchised, because leadership does not know them, nor do they appear interested in their opinions and suggestions—much less the feedback from customers these frontline employees receive daily. The leaders they report to have no idea what they are thinking, and therefore cannot bring their valuable knowledge to the table. Judy and her colleagues were never involved in the decision-making process, even though they were the ones who had all the right questions and many of the answers. If only they had been asked.

This was a case of company-wide disengagement. The CEO was disengaged from what actually was going on in the company; he and other leaders were focusing on financial issues and were essentially disengaged from the call centers, and their employees. And their clients were dissatisfied and looking to leave at their first opportunity—so they were disengaged as well.

So how *do* leaders become more engaged? It almost always has to start with a change in perspective, which isn't easy. It's not as though you can just turn a switch inside your head. One of the most challenging things for leaders is to learn how to look at things in a new light. When you are inside the system, doing the same thing day after day, year after year, it can be extremely difficult to change your perception about how you and your company are operating. You actually, in some ways, have become part of the problem.

When I interviewed Don Gogel, the CEO of Clayton Dubilier & Rice (CD&R), one of the country's oldest and most successful private equity firms, he told me, "When I visit with a CEO, the first thing I always tell them is that I have an unfair advantage over them—because I am able to look at their company with fresh eyes. I have no biases, no history of the company's past decisions or issues to cloud my vision. Therefore I can see what they don't see. That's how I am able to perceive the inherent value of these companies."[1]

Gogel offered me a great example of this fresh eyes phenomenon. In 1991, CD&R acquired the impact and laser printer business from IBM, which was starting a period of restructuring. They named this business Lexmark. "IBM's vaunted and well-deserved reputation was established through its extraordinary mainframe technology," Gogel said. "IBM product development teams operated with great discipline. For example, because the IBM mainframes needed to have exceptionally high reliability, its product developers had backup systems and redundancy for everything. They had to dual-source every component and so had to qualify two vendors. Product testing could take up to a year. Of course, when you are making mainframe computers that is the right way to do it. But when you begin making laser printers, that's another story."

Gogel explained that at the time, the printer business looked more like consumer electronics. "Hewlett Packard and several Japanese manufacturers were very strong, competing on both price and broad distribution. They were introducing new models twice a year. The nature of this competition created two very big issues for IBM. The first was cost—because IBM had been designing very reliable printers in a market that was more interested in low cost. The second was the product innovation cycle. Hewlett Packard was basically innovating two products a year, while Lexmark was on an eighteen-month cycle of new product introductions."

CD&R bought the printer business from IBM because the firm believed that it could dramatically transform the way the company operated. CD&R partners were convinced the company had great technology but needed to change the way it developed products and went to market. "Fortunately," Gogel said, "we managed to persuade Paul Curlander, the IBM vice president who designed IBM's first laser printer, to join the new company as our chief engineer. We also recruited Marvin Mann, a seasoned IBM executive who knew the business, as our first CEO. In addition, a CD&R operating partner, Chuck Ames, assumed the chairman's role and brought a great deal of industrial marketing and sales force management experience to the company. Together, they transformed Lexmark.

"Now Paul," Gogel continued, "who in 1998 became Lexmark's CEO, understood that he would have to dramatically change the product development process. He said that he would have to take the IBM product manual and encase it in a Lucite cube and put it on display. He wanted to show how important it was to avoid the 'old' playbook. Under Paul's leadership, Lexmark competed with the best manufacturers in the world on price and performance and rolled out several new products each year for both laser and then ink-jet printers. Paul became the CEO of Lexmark in 1998 and held that position until 2010.

"Notwithstanding his deep IBM roots, Marvin immediately started to change the style and culture at Lexmark, emphasizing speed and customer responsiveness. And Chuck, with his deep marketing experience, developed an industry-specific sales force that became a major competitive edge in an industry where competitors sold largely through dealers."[2]

Although it took five years to get things right, Lexmark was a great success, going public and growing to have a market capitalization of $10 billion by 2004.[3] For a variety of reasons, IBM had not seen that the printer business required different principles, strategies, and cost structures from the computer business. CD&R and the new management team were able to look at the situation in a new way. Together, they brought new insights to develop a new strategy and organization to transform the slow-moving typewriter and impact printer into an agile and fast-moving technology company.

In this case, CD&R, looking with fresh eyes, was able to see why this different approach was necessary. They made a number of changes during their years of ownership, and as a result Lexmark became a more valuable enterprise. But almost more impressive was the way the longtime

IBM engineer and the other leaders rose to the challenge. Fairly quickly, they were able to overcome years of training, change their "corporate DNA," and see the problem objectively.

What prevents leaders inside a company from doing the same thing as Gogel—and the Lexmark management team? If a private equity firm can buy a company, make fundamental changes to its operations, and sell the company for three to five times its original value in five years, why can't the leaders who are already at that company make those same changes? Do companies need to wait until they are purchased to be able to address their fundamental issues? Do they need a serious crisis in order to create the urgency to make decisions and act aggressively?

My answer is a resounding and unequivocal "No." I have seen far too many cases, both in my own personal experience and from observing businesses in general, where companies whose leaders are truly engaged generate great results.

Especially in large organizations, certain systems and programs tend to become deeply entrenched; there are things that were set in motion years ago to which no one ever gives a thought. They just become set in stone. We have to remind ourselves they are not set in stone—it only looks like stone. Learning how to see with objectivity is the essential first step, because becoming aware of the underlying disengagement within your organization is the only way to begin eliminating the many blockages— blockages that not only get in the way of you and your leaders' ability to address fundamental operational issues but also hinder their ability to carry out important, bold new strategies.

HOW CAN YOU BEGIN TO TRAIN YOURSELF TO SEE WITH FRESH EYES?

For a few days or even a week, pretend you just started the job you're now in. You're brand new to the company; you've never even seen the offices before. What would you do? How would you behave? You would likely meet lots of people in your organization and would begin to get the rhythm and pulse of the place. Because you're new, you would ask dozens of fact-finding questions, such as: "Why do we do it that way?" "Why do we do that at all?" Or "Have you considered checking with Brian to see if that works for him?" If you reengage in this way, I promise you that you will be surprised at what you discover—what you will now be able to really "see."

It's staggering how much of what goes on in a company usually remains unnoticed. If you could somehow place your company into an MRI machine and slice through it in three-dimensional detail, what do you think you would find? How do people in your organization actually spend their time, how do they set priorities, allocate resources, and make decisions? Almost certainly, this virtual "corporate MRI" would reveal many areas where the absolutely vital element of engagement is missing, the same way doctors can see vital connective tissue missing in the ligaments of your knee. They can't discern exactly why you are experiencing pain until they have a different, better way of looking at the body—a different approach to the ailment.

Because this book is not science and not a medical book, there are no exact treatments or remedies to follow. Different leaders have different personalities; their companies have unique circumstances, issues, challenges, and opportunities. Every company has its own personality, history, and trajectory.

However, this book does illustrate common areas where a lack of engagement is often causing a problem—and then provides you with my proven, practical solutions for fixing those problems—solutions based on my Five Principles of Engagement. Of course, while each chapter in this book deals with a specific topic, the reality is that all these issues are interwoven. The key to being an engaged leader is to know what these issues are, how they interrelate, and how to improve in those areas requiring the most attention.

Why Are There Snowblowers in Miami? contains the tools for engagement. You need to put these tools to work. When you do, you will see that every small change you make will give rise to others, both in your own actions and in the actions of others around you. An increase in your engagement tends to cause positive transformation in wonderful and surprising ways.

Here are the Five Principles of Engagement:

- FRESH EYES: *Learning to adopt an outsider's perspective leads to creative insight and problem solving.* By asking questions not usually asked, and seeing what's not usually seen, you can identify areas of dysfunction, recognize opportunity, and implement bold new strategies.

- CONNECTING: *Interacting with employees and customers on a regular basis is the key to success.* Authentic communication at all levels and the encouragement of feedback is how you find out what's really going on. The answer to unleashing the power of your team—and to delighting your customers—lies outside the conference room. It is astounding how much valuable information can be obtained by simply talking to the people who really know the everyday inner workings of the company. One enlightening conversation with someone like Judy at the call center is worth a hundred meetings with fellow managers, yet rarely do leaders ever ask these employees what they think. Without a doubt, the vast majority of big decisions I have made to help turn companies around had their roots in understanding what employees told me they needed in order to please their customers. I have developed techniques that guarantee better relationships between leaders of all levels and their customers.

- HOT BUTTONS: *Focusing on two or three pertinent metrics in any situation facilitates action.* It's important to present simplified targets that every employee in the company can embrace and rally around. When beginning to engage with people, keeping it simple is the best course. The surest way to get everyone on the same page is to find the relevant numbers or facts that every employee in the company can quickly understand and act on. Unbundling projects into smaller elements—getting people to really understand what the most essential factors are in any given set of circumstances—is crucial to motivating a team.

- TRANSPARENCY: *The more people know, the better they can do their jobs.* Knowledge is power, and good information flow is of the utmost importance.

Too many companies employ tools and practices that serve to convolute rather than to clarify. Information that is relevant and timely needs to be shared as widely and efficiently as possible within a company. Targeted tracking of key performance indicators is also needed, along with an accurate evaluation and full dissemination of the results.

- SPEED: *Whatever speed you are going is too slow.* When people in a large organization are not fully engaged, it creates slowness. Remember that time is the enemy in today's global marketplace. In this fast-paced world, decisions need to be made more quickly and executed in shorter time cycles. It's vital to get quick wins, learn rapidly from failures, and learn to be comfortable with constant change. Like successful start-ups, you need to have the ability to shift almost instantly to meet changing demands. Waiting is never an option; companies cannot assume they have endless time to evaluate, plan, and launch new initiatives.

These Five Principles make up your toolkit—or they could be called your building blocks—for engaging. They are the foundation of my leadership techniques and advice—from how to cure complacency to how to radically improve the suffocating, never-ending stream of meetings.

Every company has its own unique set of issues and challenges, and some aspects of this book may be more applicable to your situation than others. One issue that all leaders agree on is that they do not have enough time, and the culprit is meetings. There are invariably too many; they are too long and too poorly run, and relatively little gets decided. So before anything else, we're going to take a look at how changing the way you hold company meetings can begin the process of engagement and produce extraordinary results.

CHAPTER TWO

STOPPING THE MEETING MADNESS

"The problem is never how to get new, innovative
thoughts into your mind, but how to get old ones out."

—Dee Hock, Visa founder

So what happens after you have identified all the places
where engagement is missing in your company? The key
is to move from assessment to action. I have found there
are always ways to begin to fix things—whether the solutions are large or small. Never balk at the prospect of making what may seem like a minor improvement; implement
enough "small" changes and suddenly you have a whole
organizational shift on your hands!

A good place to begin is to recapture or reignite the
potential for success that already exists in the capabilities of
the people who work there—to free up your team members
so they can operate at maximum capacity. One way to free
up your team is to get rid of or reinvent systems and processes that are holding them back—things that are getting
in the way of your people doing their job well.

The Tyranny of Meetings

As every person reading this book knows, there is no greater detriment to productivity than the way meetings are used in companies. Because meetings are the one aspect of company life that leaders and followers universally criticize, I decided it makes the most sense to start here—to show how a few simple fixes can quickly improve your level of engagement.

A few years ago, I was leading a team on a consulting project. My team spent significant amounts of time with leaders throughout the organization to understand what they thought their problems were. One night as I was leaving the office, I asked Dave, one of the senior vice presidents, if he could meet with me the next day. Somewhat apologetically, he told me he couldn't meet me until 6:00 p.m.

"I've got a big meeting all morning, followed by a lunch meeting, then I'm going to my three o'clock, then I have a conference call to get ready for my five o'clock," he said, pulling out a printed version of his Outlook calendar to show me. There was absolutely no blank space anywhere on it. It looked as if someone had reproduced a page out of a densely written novel and overlaid it with dozens of rectangles. "I'm always completely booked up with these #%&! meetings," he complained.

"Doesn't leave much time to do your job," I said.

He looked at me and laughed ruefully. "Welcome to my life!"

Like so many others I've met throughout my career, Dave was constantly frustrated about not having time to get any work done. He had no time to think, or talk to anyone besides the people who were in these meetings.

His company was not doing well (which of course was why my team was there), and its poor performance had resulted mostly in—guess what? More meetings to address their problems.

Meetings comprise the vast majority of time spent for everyone except the employees at the lowest levels of the company. When I ran large companies, I estimated that more than 65 percent of my time was scheduled for me, not by me. A friend unfamiliar with business practices asked me one time, "How can this be, if you are running the company? Don't you control everything?" But the truth is that the more senior you are, the more you are at the mercy of meetings.

When I was CEO of American Express Bank, in December I would automatically receive a set-in-stone schedule of mandatory corporate meetings for the coming year—monthly business reviews, annual planning reviews, management evaluation reviews, etc. So who generates this calendar? No one really knows. It's built into the system. Plus, individual departments are able to schedule meetings. This meeting schedule just exists—a fact of life, a machine on autopilot.

In fact, the majority of the people attending meetings have limited control regarding their own attendance. If someone higher up says they need to be there, they need to be there whether it is a waste of their time or not. And the managers at the top are so stuck in the "meetings habit," that they rarely consider the actual impact on individuals in the company. While everyone knows the general subject matter of the meeting, the specifics of what is to be discussed and decided are often not disclosed in advance. Usually you're not entirely sure why you're going or what the real purpose of the meeting is. Right from the start, the roller-coaster ride begins, and most people reading this book probably identify with this ride.

Meetings are generally scheduled for an hour, when in reality a fraction of that time would suffice. Of the ten or more people who attend a typical meeting, often several of them call a conference call number to participate. The first ten minutes are taken up with chatting, getting organized, figuring out who is dialing in, and getting everyone settled. Typically, a PowerPoint presentation ("the deck") is used in meetings, and a printout of it is handed out to the participants at the beginning. The leader, using the projection screen or the document itself, usually reads the deck to the followers (as if for some reason, they are not able to read it themselves) and leads the discussion. Normally there is an agenda on the first page of the deck, which is often in the form of a table of contents and may include a "next steps" page—which almost always calls for additional meetings. In spite of the meeting being an hour long, rarely is there sufficient time to get through all the pages in the deck. Invariably, someone goes off topic for fifteen minutes, and no one ever stops that person with a "Thanks, but we are not here to talk about that subject." The last five minutes of the meeting usually involve rushing to get through to the last page, because most people are packing up and getting ready to go to their next meeting. As anyone can see, this is clearly a broken process.

Increasingly, conference calls are as common and plentiful as meetings (because you can attend from anywhere) and are run the same way, except that most participants have a tendency to "multitask" and are often reading and answering their email with their phones on mute. Some people—wearing headsets—even do their dishes, clean their floors, or floss their teeth during calls. Clearly, these heads are not in the game—a fact that becomes all too evident when these people ultimately unmute their phones and offer a response to something that was covered ten minutes earlier. Oops.

What really happens in most meetings? What is the substance? In my experience, 80 percent of the typical meeting is spent looking back or reviewing history ("This is what happened; this is why we think it happened") with comparisons to the performance of previous periods and budgets. In meetings where operating results are discussed, there is little insight as to why the financial results are what they are ("We are not exactly sure why this year's numbers are lower than budget, but if this year's numbers are better than last year's, we're doing okay." Or "If this year's numbers are worse than last year's, we'll have to find ways to improve."). The discussion often focuses on either the past or present, while little time is spent talking about specific steps to drive outcomes in the future. Often, there is debate regarding the facts, with people falling over one another trying to explain why poor results are really not that bad. Sometimes when I am listening to these discussions I am reminded of the old Irish joke, "If three guys tell you you're drunk, sit down."

Information presented in meetings is highly summarized and is geared to gain acceptance of whatever the "ask" is. Seldom are viable alternatives and choices presented. The tough questions ("What other options did we consider?" "Do we really understand the causal factors that created the situation in the first place?") are hardly ever posed, in part because people want to be perceived as team players and don't want to challenge anyone, and also because they have not given sufficient thought to alternatives—since they're sold on the recommendation. Recommendations that start out as "aggressive and bold" when initially conceived are frequently diluted and/or rejected because "we'll never get this approved by our EVP." So the top leaders never get to see what people are really thinking.

Meetings tend to wear people out. It's not just the time spent in the meeting itself. A significant amount of time is required to research and prepare the deck. The pace of meetings is relentless, the conversations are fairly predictable, and there is little hope that the process will change—much like being on a treadmill. So a sense of futility, resignation, and acceptance of this as a way of life sets in—in other words, people begin to disengage. It's very hard under these circumstances to expect leaders to step up and take initiative. Dave, the senior vice president with the overloaded Outlook calendar, was very well intentioned, but he was out of gas and had obviously pretty much checked out.

Perhaps the most important problem with meetings is that very little is ever decided. Unless there is a hard deadline (e.g., a contract that has to be signed by next Friday), it is rare for any meaningful decision to be made during meetings. And because no decision gets made, follow-up meetings are scheduled, creating an endless string of additional meetings. The overabundance of meetings and lack of decisions make any real initiative almost impossible; everyone is continuously in reaction mode. The lower-level employees are not even a part of the equation, except for the fact that they can't reach any of their bosses, who are all in meetings! Most of you reading this book can relate to Dave; your calendar probably looks a lot like his. It can often seem as though the meetings are running the people instead of the people running the meetings.

The New Meetings Model: Creating Time for People to Solve Problems

One of the first ways for a leader to truly engage and initiate change is to rethink the entire meeting process. It's truly amazing how most people accept the inefficacy of the way meetings are run in most companies, as if the process is unalterable. The objective of the new meetings model described here is to dramatically reduce the number of meetings while at the same time improving the quality and substance of what happens during and after the meetings. Of course, overhauling the meeting process must begin at the top with the senior leadership team of the company, largely because their behavior completely influences the behavior of the rest of the organization. One of the reasons to begin with fixing meetings is that it so clearly demonstrates to everyone in the organization what engagement can feel like; when the meeting process is successful, it will make leaders eager to move on to the other areas where they can employ the principles of engagement.

The following are three basic components for productive meetings:

1. **Issue rules for meetings** that everyone must follow, which include reducing the quantity of meetings, the duration of meetings, and the number of participants at meetings.

2. **Create an ownership system** for meetings to inspire

good management and to ensure that all parties are vested in the new process.

3. **Define the types of meetings and their objectives**—and the expectations of what should happen for each type.

RULES FOR MEETINGS

Process

Preparation is critical to having efficient and effective meetings. Whenever possible, relevant information should be sent to the attendees at least forty-eight hours prior to the meeting. This document—whatever its form—should be brief, and the first item on page one should state the purpose of the meeting as well as the anticipated outcome (making a decision, sharing information, etc.). Attendees must read this information in advance, so that the meeting time can be kept to a minimum. It is vital that you do NOT read this material during the actual meeting. This one step alone will substantially alter the nature and duration of meetings.

The initial portion of the meeting is designed for attendees to ask questions, to raise issues, and to ensure everyone has the information they need to satisfy the meeting's stated objective. The discussion itself must focus on making sure that the stated objective is fulfilled, while still adjourning on time. If specific questions come up that require additional work (information, analysis, etc.), a follow-up document should be sent out in response. Several days later, a short conference call can be held to answer any questions and make the decision. It's not necessary to hold another meeting to finalize the issue, given the effectiveness of the original discussion and the specific follow-ups provided.

Just by following these two simple process rules, what would likely have been two one-hour meetings has become a thirty-minute meeting with a ten-minute follow-up call. That's an improvement of 66 percent from the typical approach right there!

Attendees

If the purpose of the meeting is to make a decision, the only people who should attend the meeting are those who have a vested interest and a vote. It is their responsibility to make sure their respective staffs have briefed them so they can be knowledgeable and up to date on the issues and ready to make an informed decision. Having multiple people from the same department attend a meeting (sometimes there are as many as three others) is a waste of manpower and another example of how meetings can reduce the company's effective capacity. By reducing the number of attendees at each meeting, the 66 percent efficiency improvement increases even further, due to the amount of time saved by those individuals who are no longer required to attend—very grateful individuals who can be working on other things.

Time Allocated for a Meeting

Instead of all meetings being one hour long—the default setting in most companies—meetings should be targeted to last thirty minutes, unless there are specific reasons for more time. The duration of a meeting should be based on need, not habit. This change alone will make a radical impact on your overall time spent in meetings. A "Meeting Czar" (see explanation in the next section) should determine whether the topic would be best served with a meeting, a call, or simply by distributing materials. Calls are more productive than meetings because they tend to be shorter (with less kibitzing) and because people don't need to physically spend time walking back and forth to the meeting. And when short calls are run well by the Czar, there will be less multitasking by the participants. People will be too focused on the call to feel the urge to answer email messages and texts during the meeting (or doing their dishes!). Another benefit.

OWNERSHIP OF MEETINGS—THE MEETING CZAR

As we know all too well, the free-for-all model—where anyone can set up a meeting and invite anyone they choose—does not work. In fact, this may be the biggest meeting madness culprit. Instead, a governance approach should be adopted to ensure the meeting model is properly implemented and aggressively managed. "Managed" is the operative word here because without proper management the meeting process tends to take on a life of its own. So you need to manage this problem the same way you deal with every other problem you encounter. Put someone in charge.

Central to the meetings model is ownership. On a rotational basis, each member of the leadership team will assume the responsibility for "owning" all meetings for this group for the period of time agreed to by the team, usually two weeks at a time. As interim Meeting Czar, this person will: (1) approve all meeting requests for this group; (2) have the final decision on attendees for each meeting; (3) determine meeting type and length, based on content and expected outcome; (4) make sure premeeting documents are distributed forty-eight hours prior to the meeting; (5) lead the actual meeting and keep within the allotted time frame; and (6) ensure the meeting goal is achieved. In other words, manage meetings the way you would manage any other process in your company.

I know at this point you're probably saying to yourself, "That's sounds like a lot of work when I already don't have time to do my job. Will having a Czar really change anything? And if so, why don't we just hire someone to be the permanent Meeting Czar and let that person do it?" These are good questions, and here are my answers.

Think of this as making an investment in running your business in an entirely different manner. In order to stop the crushing weight of meetings, to change the current course, an investment of time is needed. And if it's done well, using the Meeting Czar model will not take up as much time as you may think. You can't hire people to do this because they will have no skin in the game, and more important, you and your team members would have no respect for this dedicated position, so nothing would really change. Each of the leaders on the team, in a self-policing manner, needs to make these hard decisions as Czar on behalf of your team— knowing that in two weeks, someone else on this team will have that responsibility. This becomes a shared responsibility of the team, and you all have a stake in making this work well.

Let's say there are ten people on the management team, and each leader takes a turn at being Czar for two weeks, so that after five months each leader has had a turn. Over the course of this period, interesting things begin to happen, and together you all begin to learn how to operate better. You will see how different leaders behave as Czar. By the time the third Czar takes over in week five, all aspects of meetings will have improved. The team will continue to develop a rhythm during this initial five-month cycle, and the process will become more and more natural to everyone. Decisions will be made more quickly. Team members will find they have substantially more time—and everyone will agree this is a great payoff. A side benefit is that the working relationships among team members will also improve; each rotating Meeting Czar will be able to share valuable leadership insights with the other members of the team.

Once the company leadership team feels like they have found their own rhythm, it's time to move the process down to the next level of management. Members of middle management will have already begun to see the effects of this new meeting practice by observing how the top team has changed in a positive way, and this will encourage them to move forward with greater certainty and conviction. By the end of the first year of implementation, decisions will be made more quickly, and a substantial amount of valuable time will be created for leaders at all levels in the company. This time can be refocused on employees and customers, which I will discuss in later chapters. So as you can see, there are multiple benefits to adopting the new meetings model. This level of engagement will be apparent not only to everyone on the leadership team but also to many others throughout the company. This builds a great foundation for working on the other principles while it frees up the entire organization so that it can accomplish so much more.

DEFINING MEETINGS AND THEIR OBJECTIVES

The third element of the new meetings model is to clearly define the types of meetings and the expectations for each. While there are many types of meetings, here are some examples of the most common and how to define them for your team.

Financial Reviews

Most managers have access to financial reports that tell them how their unit, department, division, or company did this month, this year, and what the comparisons are to last year and to the budget. For a financial review meeting to be valuable, it has to explore one or more of these three questions: How were the results achieved?; Why are the results different from what was expected?; and most important, What—if anything—will we do differently for the balance of the year? This assessment is normally a combination of fact and subjective judgment. Often there is disagreement about the explanation of the results.

Asking the question "So what, now what?" can help convert the how and why into actionable plans. Presentations often end without anyone having a clear understanding of the significance of the findings ("So what?") and what specific next steps and actions should be taken ("Now what?"). This is a very useful clarifying tool. It is vitally important that the leadership team understands and agrees to a revised plan based on their understanding of the results and the potential impact for the balance of the year. The key here is to spend the majority of time in these types of meetings on the "So what, now what?" questions. This is the only way to make sure necessary changes are identified and implemented.

Weekly Staff Meetings

Obviously it is important for the team to meet regularly to update each other on important initiatives and to review both the good and the bad news. But if each member spoke in a highly focused manner for three minutes (even allowing for some extra deliberation or elaboration within the group), this meeting should take forty-five minutes.

Subject Matter Meetings

These meetings are not homogeneous but cover a variety of areas. One example might be a discussion about the need to open a new operating center based on the company's anticipated business growth. Normally, this kind of subject might entail dozens of meetings over a period of months, often because individual departments are building their own cases.

A topic like this requires level setting: Has the business case been made that we need a new operating center? (If not, why are we spending the time to determine if Des Moines is the right city?); Do we understand the timing regarding when the center needs to be live (this will narrow choices and focus decision making)?; Have we considered other alternatives?; and so on.

More preparation with individuals across the organization can produce a document that clearly states the problem, the opportunity, the choices and options, the timing, and the possible financial outcomes. Giving people this information and allowing for questions at key intervals, either with short meetings or conference calls, organized with a tight agenda, can greatly facilitate this process.

When all the preparation work has been executed properly, the final meeting—scheduled by the Meeting Czar—should be only to hear any final questions or issues and have the leadership team make the decision.

Stand-Up Meetings

When the circumstances call for it, this is a great way to have a quick meeting (twenty minutes or less). As the name implies, everyone stands up at the meeting so that no one gets too comfortable (in many cases the chairs are either removed or turned to face the wall). These meetings are ideally suited for situations where everyone needs to be aware of recent status updates and other new issues. Supply chain leaders often use these so that everyone in the group is fully aware of raw materials, inventory, etc., and so that they can highlight problems and immediate fixes. You state your business, listen to the others, and go back to your job. Done.

My main point is that you need to think about meetings the way you would think about any other activity in the company—especially because this one sucks up so much time. Creating structure, process, accountability, and a rotational leader (the Czar) will show everyone in the organization how serious you are about cracking this problem, which is a virtual sinkhole when it comes to wasting productive hours. Changing meetings is where leaders should start because improvement in this area can make such an enormous difference—and can very quickly provide people with time to pursue more valuable activities.

Email and Texting: The Illusion of Efficiency

It's not just actual meetings that are a time suck. On a recent flight back to New York from Chicago (two and a half hours) I turned my phone back on after we touched down and found that I had received eighty-seven email messages and five voicemails while I was in flight. I shudder to think what will happen on my next flight to Tokyo. Email and texting are on the fast track to compete with meetings as the major consumer of our time. And I'm not including all the junk mail, spam, and other items that are typically caught in filters. I'm just talking about the stuff that gets through. What explains this tonnage of email?

There are several patterns I've noticed, and many of these relate to other issues. First is the need to cc everyone directly, indirectly, and tangentially related to the subject. While that is not necessarily bad, each time one of the individuals respond, they hit "reply all"—cc'ing everyone. Very quickly, the original email generates dozens more, with every response somewhat out of sync because generally each response arrives at the same approximate time as everyone else's. Some of the people included should definitely be on the email list, but often the others are only included to cover your ass (CYA), so that everyone on the list knows your position; ensure you do not leave someone out, potentially offending them (even though they complain they are barraged with email); laziness, and other reasons.

Second, email messages in general are too long. It is much easier to just type a stream of consciousness than to take a little extra time to succinctly write the essence of your point.

Third, it is usually unclear what the "ask" is. Do you

want a decision? Is this for information purposes only? Is there something I need to follow up on? Very often, you can read a long email not knowing what the expectation of the sender is until the end or, in some cases, not even at the end. (And too often a problem could be solved in real time in a few minutes with a simple phone call.)

And then of course there is the torrent of texting—a relatively new form of communication but one that is swiftly taking over all other modes of communication. I've been in presentations where individuals are texting each other during the meeting. Content can range from "Do you believe they are actually saying this?" to "No way we should go forward with this idea." to "Where did they find this guy?" and on and on.

So the obvious question is, When are the majority of these email and text messages read and responded to? Amazingly, the answer is, usually, during meetings. Some people may be bored with the discussion in the meeting and are looking for a better use of their time, and others are aware that the sheer volume of messages must be responded to. It's interesting to watch how people do this. Some have their phone glued to their hand and are overtly reading and responding. Others, attempting to be more stealthy, hold the phone surreptitiously under the table. Advanced practitioners will keep one eye on their phone and the other looking at someone in the meeting. But even in the best cases, their attention is divided, and they are not fully "present" for either activity. And so, in situations where information sharing and true transparency are paramount, these supposed information tools are actually inhibiting rather than helping the exchanges.

One day, I had a phone pitch scheduled with a potential

client; five of my team members were going to be in on the call.

"I have a hard stop at 12:30," I emailed the colleague who was setting it up. (No surprise, I had another meeting scheduled for then!)

He responded, "Me too. I have a super hard stop @ 12:30 p.m. as well . . . let's keep this email channel open to communicate to each other during pitch."

I was leading the pitch, with my other team members contributing ideas on the call. Naturally I was not looking at my phone because I was concentrating on speaking and listening to everyone. After the call, another colleague of mine, Frank, called me to say I had "crushed" it (meaning the sales pitch). When I finally looked at my phone, I saw there were a dozen email messages and texts that had been sent back and forth among the people on my team, all sent during the phone pitch, about who should say what on the call (Is this multitasking, or multidistracting?). I said to Frank, "I don't think I would have been able to focus on the call if I had been texting and emailing during the pitch."

We as a society have not really figured out yet how to tame the beast of communication technology. When it comes to business communications, more is not always better. The email/texting tsunami is an ongoing issue, and it's an addiction difficult to curb (although we should try).

I have begun implementing a simple tactic recently, which I can see is having an impact in the meetings I attend; though by no means is it solving the larger problem. Simply stated, I have banned the use of laptops and smartphones in meetings. I've told people that they may answer their phone (call) only if there is an emergency, and that they should let everyone in their group know what the rule is. Of course, some complain quite adamantly that they need access to information during the meeting—and I agree that there are some instances when emailing, texting, or checking something on a laptop is relevant and helpful to the discussion. But I believe that preventing Google search, shopping on Amazon, placing bets on FanDuel, and other distractions outweighs any value that access to the Internet during a meeting offers.

If you make the effort to implement the new meetings model, you're looking at an improvement of at least 66 percent in meeting time and an additional, unknowable amount of increased efficiency and positive outcomes. Most important, you will now have the time and energy to interact with employees and customers in ways that were not possible before. It's certainly worth making this relatively small investment to gain so much.

CHAPTER THREE

OUT OF THE MOUTHS OF WINDOW WASHERS

*"I suppose leadership at one time meant muscles;
but today it means getting along with people."*

—Mahatma Gandhi

It was 8 a.m. on a Wednesday morning in London, and I was sitting at my desk. There was no one else in the office yet. It was 1988 and my third day on a new assignment, which was to run the card, travel, and traveler's checks business of American Express for the United Kingdom and Ireland. I had been sent there to turn around the business, and it was a great opportunity to live and work in a different country.

Suddenly I felt a presence and turned around to find a window washer setting up to clean the interior windows in the office. A bit startled, I said, "Hi, my name is Steve, what's yours?"

After a brief pause, he said nervously, "My name is John." He was a short man, on the older side, wearing blue coveralls with one suspender down, a newspaper stuck in his pocket, and a cigarette hanging out of his mouth. He had a thick Cockney accent.

"It's nice to meet you, John." I said. "How long have you been washing windows here?" A look of pride came over his face. "Twenty-five years, sir." Then he asked, "Are you the new guv'nor, sir?"

"Yes, I guess I am the new governor," I replied, not quite sure how to pronounce it like John did.

"It's good you're here," said John solemnly, "the other guv'nor wasn't doing a good job."

"How do you know that?" I asked him.

John said, "I go into people's offices to wash the windows, but they don't see me, it's like I'm not there. I hear what they say to the people in their office and when they're on the phone—and they say everything, because like I said, they don't really see me—I'm only the window washer." Flabbergasted, I asked John if he wanted to join me for a cup of coffee, to which he—after hesitating a little—said okay.

We spent the next forty-five minutes having an amazing conversation, at the end of which he said, "I'm sorry, guv', but I have to get back to work or I'll be in big trouble with the boss." I thanked him and asked if he would like to have a cup of coffee in a month, and he said yes.

After that initial encounter, I met John for coffee on a regular basis, went to a pub after work to have a beer with him a couple of times, and invited him to our Christmas party. My leadership team, who would occasionally see John leaving my office, could not understand why I would waste my time talking to the window washer.

Here is the point of the story: I learned more in my first meeting with John than I could have ever learned reviewing reports, or even talking to my team. In spite of the limited schooling he had had, he was extremely perceptive about what was going on in the business. Not surprisingly, he didn't have the vocabulary to describe things in professional terms, but he had the smarts to accurately diagnose business issues and even had helpful insight about people on the team. Thinking back, I've always felt so fortunate to have had this experience, because it reinforced my belief in the value of reaching out to people at all levels. Every once in a while when I'm meeting with people at the lower levels in an organization, I recall my conversation with John and other similar conversations I have had and realize how much I learned from them.

Why don't more leaders reach out like this? There are a number of possible explanations, but I think it is more a matter of will than skill. Of course, there are some people who are born introverts; interacting with different kinds of people does not come naturally to them, and they prefer to stay within the confines of their familiar circles. And all leaders are busy—time being by far their scarcest resource—and meeting with the working staff is obviously time consuming. It's hard to find time for any kind of face-to-face interaction if there is no clear, definable benefit to it.

But there is usually more to it than this. Some leaders are insecure. They feel nervous about letting their hair down— some are fearful of being judged, and some are uneasy asking people open-ended questions. When you engage in a real conversation—one that's not scripted, where you are communicating in the moment—you never know when you could find yourself in a conversation that might make you uncomfortable. Insecure leaders might be afraid they won't know the answers to people's questions, or that the answers will be something the staff won't want to hear.

Another reason for this lack of engagement between people at the top and those at the bottom is that a lot of leaders have inflated egos. *I'm a vice president, they think, why should I waste my time speaking with a salesclerk, an assembly line worker, or the cleaning lady in a hotel? I don't need to speak with those folks. I'm an important executive. They can't help me get ahead; they're too far below me.* This may be a more subconscious motivation, but I have seen this attitude often among leaders.

There are undoubtedly many other reasons why leaders do not take the time and trouble to speak to lower-level employees, but one thing is certain: They are losing a lot by not engaging with these folks. The information that can be mined is like intelligence the CIA would drool over if a spy could get it during a covert operation. And talking to a window washer—or a receptionist, or an assistant—is a lot easier than going undercover in Iran.

A few months ago, I was in the checkout line of a major retailer and could not help overhearing the conversation between the customer in front of me and the salesclerk behind the cash register. "I bought this shirt online, but I'd like to return it here," said the customer.

The answer from the clerk was, "No, you need to return it online where you bought it."

The customer said, "I don't understand—it's the same shirt that you're selling right over there on the rack—why do I have to return it online when I'm standing here now in the store?"

"It is our policy that you must return the item where you bought it," the clerk responded, "and since you bought it online, that is where you need to return it."

Visibly annoyed, the customer said, "I'd like to speak to the manager."

"She is out this afternoon," was the reply.

"Okay, I'll return this stupid shirt online, and you can be sure I will never buy anything from your company again," grumbled the customer, to which—not surprisingly—the clerk said nothing.

There are many possible "logical" explanations to explain this company's policy: separate supply chains, inconsistent channel pricing, separate profit and loss statements for the retail and online divisions, IT systems that are not able to see transactions in various selling channels, etc. But whatever the explanation is, it was not relevant to either the customer or the salesclerk at that moment. All either of them knew was the frustration stemming from a ridiculous rule.

Who in "corporate" was even aware this return policy problem existed? And if they were aware, would they care? Are the various negative impacts of this issue addressed in any of the meetings held at this company? Does this interaction show up in any of the reports they look at? The likely answer is no, and that's a problem in and of itself.

I submit that if senior leaders in this company visited stores, spoke to cashiers and salespeople on the floor, and observed the sales process in action, they'd invariably witness these types of interactions. And I truly believe they would go back to their team, explain the situation, and ask that it be corrected quickly. (If not, the company has a very different kind of problem—having to do with that particular leader.)

The good news about engaging with people at entry levels or "on the front lines" is that it is not hard to do. Although it does take time, commitment, and the willingness to look at situations with fresh eyes, it's amazing to me that so few leaders make the effort. And yet, I continue to witness this form of disengagement everywhere I go.

I came across a good example recently when I was at the airport in Atlanta returning a rental car to Hertz. I happen to have a Hertz platinum card that affords me a special service where they drive you back to the terminal from the rental car center; this saves a lot of time. This is a great convenience because it's about a twenty-minute trip on the train at Hartsfield International Airport.

When I drove up to Hertz on this particular occasion, there did not seem to be much activity. The driver who got in the car with me to take me to the airport was a middle-aged woman named Jenny.

I turned to her and said, "I've been coming here every week for the past two months, why are you not so busy today?"

"Oh, yeah," Jenny said. "That's 'cause they changed the valet program."

"What's the valet program?"

"Hon', you got the platinum card, so you automatically get the service. But it used to be, for certain customers, they would run them back to the terminal for nothing." She went on to tell me that they had recently decided to start charging people twenty-five dollars for the valet service, and no one wanted the service now.

"Why did they do that?"

"They wanted to make more money . . . but this is the largest Hertz counter in the United States—baby they're makin' so much money, they don't need to make that much more money." Jenny was obviously indignant and letting loose on this subject, having found a willing ear. "I mean someone's taking a car out for two or three weeks, what's the big deal with giving them a free ride to the airport? . . . And you know what really pisses me off?" (And I knew she was going to tell me without any further encouragement on my part.) "If a vet rents the car, they should take him to the airport. These guys are fightin' for our country, givin' their lives, comin' back all messed up, with PTSD and all, and we can't even give him a ride to the airport? . . . And then we got a woman with three kids and a stroller, all by herself, she's tryin' to make ends meet—they don't give her a ride to the airport?"

I said to Jenny, "It sounds like you know a lot about this stuff."

She looked at me with a big smile. "Honey," she said, "I see everything. I see what's going on."

"Do you ever tell anybody about these ideas?"

"Oh, yes. I sure do. They say, 'Miss Jones, you sure have the best ideas.'"

"What do they tell you to do with them?"

"They tell me to put 'em in the suggestion box. So I say to them, 'Wait a minute, I put it in the suggestion box, you take all the credit, I get nothin'—that don't make a whole lot of sense."

I asked her, "Well, has anyone ever come down to spend time with you?"

"Oh yeah!" Jenny said. "Some of the supervisors come over . . . they always come over to me because they know I have the suggestions, and they tell me to put it in the suggestion box. But I'm not doin' this anymore. They don't even buy me a sandwich!"

"So you want to get compensated for this?" I asked her.

"Hell no, but at least buy me a sandwich!"

"Did you ever ask them why they don't buy you a sandwich?"

"Yeah."

"Well, what did they say?"

"They said, 'If I buy you a sandwich, then I have to buy everybody a sandwich.' So I said, 'Well, tell everybody to put their suggestions in the suggestion box, and buy everybody a sandwich!'"

I had to laugh at this, Jenny was so spot on in her assessment.

"Does anyone from corporate headquarters, the suits, ever come down here?" I asked.

"Hell no, they don't wanna come down here, in the garage . . . you know, it's hot, it's dark, noisy, cars are movin' around . . . they don't wanna see what's goin' on here." She shook her head. "Here's how I see it. Somebody rents a car here for like, five days—it's probably $600, $700—and we're makin' money on that. If we bring them home in the valet service for free, they're gonna go tell all their friends. And then we're gonna rent more cars. Why won't they do that? Don't they see we'd make more money than this? Who needs the twenty-five dollars?!"

This woman had really nailed it. She understood so much, and it made her crazy that no one cared. We were just about to pull up at the curb at that point. I turned to Jenny, and I said to her, "You know Jenny, you are really smart. You really know what you are talking about, and I wish they would listen to you." I couldn't help wishing I could have somehow magically transported the CEO of Hertz into this car with Jenny and me so he could hear what she had to say.

In 2009 CBS produced a television show called Undercover Boss, based on a program that had originated in Britain. The US version premiered in February 2010, has strong ratings, and is now in its seventh season.[1] Each episode features a high-ranking executive or the owner of a corporation going undercover—posing as an entry-level employee in his or her own company in order to experience what their employees and their customers live with every day.

Using makeup and other forms of deception, the executives alter their appearance and assume an alias and fictional backstory. They spend approximately a week undercover working in various areas of their company's operations, with different jobs and in most cases a different location each day. The CEOs who go undercover in this show seem astonished to find that they have employees who care so much about dealing with customers and their concerns; who understand what is going right and wrong within the company; and who, in many cases, have solutions. Yet it takes a production studio—supplying false identities, physical disguises, and other techniques—to enable these leaders to experience this.

Why not just do it without the disguise? Why is the idea of the CEO mixing with the people at "the bottom" so exotic it can become a show that runs for seven seasons? One reason is this: The boss thinks that unless she is incognito, she will not get an accurate picture if she asks questions as the boss. When people see the boss coming, they tend to scurry around and try to put a good face on everything. Alternatively, employees like window washers are virtually invisible to most people in the company. John, the window washer in London, had been treated like a piece of furniture for years (sometimes I think he talked to me out of sheer stupefaction that anyone had noticed him).

When I interviewed Andrew Florance, the founder and CEO of CoStar Group (the leading provider of commercial real estate information) he told me, "When you go into an organization, you can always tell when it is one where no one at the top talks to people at the bottom, because people tend to flip out when you talk to someone they don't expect you to talk to. 'Wait a minute, you have to go through me!' they'll say. And I say, 'No, actually I don't.'" Florance told me about the time he once put on the janitor's outfit for Halloween. "I put on the hat, I put on the whole gear, got the trash can and the mop, and I walked around the building," he said. "And it was amazing. We've had the same janitors for years. And yet, here I was, and nobody saw me. I mopped the floor, took the trash cans out. No one recognized me. It made me appreciate how important it is to say hi to the janitor."[2]

Getting into the good habit of talking to staff on all levels is something that has to happen from the top down—senior leaders instilling this idea in the leaders below them and so on—so that the person at the bottom isn't scared to tell the truth about what is going on. Unless people feel that they are valued and protected, that they are able to offer their opinion without any possible reprisals or any negativity, they are going to clam up and play it safe. They will merely put on a good front for the boss. On one hand, it's hard to say whether the clerk at the clothing store would have revealed the issue she was having regarding the return of an item if the CEO had walked in the door at that moment.

On the other hand, would Jenny Jones have told the top boss exactly what she told me? You better believe she would have!

Leaders, you don't have to put on makeup and a clever disguise to find out what's going on. I'm proposing a much easier solution—just do it! Get out of your office. Visit people and talk to them; make this a priority. It doesn't have to be the window washer, janitor, or driver; the stories in this chapter are merely examples. There is no set checklist of people in specific jobs to whom you must talk. But no matter whom you run into in your workplace during your daily routine—people you might not ever have talked to before—why not stop and chat, buy them a cup of coffee or even a sandwich?

HERE ARE SOME THINGS YOU CAN DO TO GET STARTED:

- Accept as fact that you will learn a lot about your company's inner workings and how the company interacts with customers by talking to as many employees as you can.
- Be natural in your interactions. Don't be stiff or contrived; try not to show any awareness of the differences in your levels. Speak to these employees the way you would if you were with your friends playing golf or going to a movie; or if you were talking to someone you don't know at your gym.
- Go alone when you go on these "connecting missions"—you don't need an entourage or an advance team to schedule and/or "manage" these interactions. Just be yourself.
- Take notes—and let the folks you're meeting see you taking notes. It will show them you are sincere in your interest.
- Report back to your team on what you've learned. I promise you that you will always have items to report back on that can be fixed, improved, implemented.
- Make sure these follow-up items are implemented. The best way to convince people in the organization that you are listening is for them to see clear changes resulting from their feedback. They will connect the dots between your conversation with them and the resulting changes. This will of course encourage them—and everyone else—to be more open.
- As you go about your daily routine, sprinkle comments here and there that illustrate your new engagement level, such as, "I visited with Jane in the accounts payable department, and she had some great ideas about how we can speed up paying our bills." When you do this everyone will realize you are serious about this kind of engaging.
- Most important, have fun and enjoy this. It is really great to get to know the people in your organization, especially the ones who really care about their customers, and their jobs.

CHAPTER FOUR

THE IMPORTANCE OF FOCUS: HOT BUTTONS AND THE QUICK WIN

"Don't judge each day by the harvest
you reap but by the seeds that you plant."

—Robert Louis Stevenson

People in most companies are so busy and preoccupied with the complex internal processes and rhythms of the organization that they sometimes entirely lose sight of what's going on outside their own offices. Awash in a sea of reports and entrenched systems, they often operate by rote. Remember the saying, "You can't see the forest for the trees"? Well, for most leaders, it's just the opposite: They can't see the trees for the forest. In other words, juggling the same set of problems and operational matters over a protracted period of time causes people to behave in a highly predictable, programmatic manner and can make them miss important things that are right under their noses.

I have found that one of the keys to bringing about genuine change is to keep it simple—in two specific ways.

The first is about discovering the right "focus"; that is, identifying the specific two to three elements most relevant to your company's particular circumstances. Getting people to really understand what is essential in a given situation is crucial to moving them to action. The second area where simplification can be constructive involves paring down items for which you need approval. If you unbundle requests into smaller components, you can often get that approval more quickly, and much more easily. Of course, as I said in chapter 1, you will need fresh eyes to begin doing either of these things.

Hot Buttons

Leaders, and in many cases the rank-and-file employees as well, are continuously bombarded with information. Email, printed material, posters, videos, etc., are disseminated from many departments—departments that usually do not coordinate with each other regarding messaging, timing, and distribution. There is always a lot of overlap in the information, and rarely is it efficiently prioritized. A major consequence of this deluge is that it is very hard for people to know what's really important, especially as it relates to individuals doing their jobs. It's like trying to locate the key to a specific door with a hundred keys on the key ring.

How do you identify the two or three critical levers that will make a difference in the business? How do you find those few items that everyone will "get"—and present them so that people understand how it impacts their specific roles or responsibilities? The answer is to narrow the focus—to use what I call "hot buttons." I've long been a big believer in these. Used properly, hot buttons can really unleash an organization.

Here's an example. About a year ago I became chairman of a large used car company that had just been purchased by a private equity fund. For years the company had been highly compartmentalized, and very little financial information was shared between the various departments. I understood, as did our investors, that our financial performance depended on a few key metrics: the number of cars we sold and the gross margin we earned; the level of credit losses we had for unpaid loans; our management of the inventory of cars; and the interest cost on the debt we incurred to buy and then finance the cars we sold to our customers.

As soon as the deal closed, we began holding weekly leadership meetings. In week two, I asked the team, "How many days of inventory do we have?"

"That's complicated," was the answer. What followed was an extended conversation about all the issues relating to inventory. At no time during the conversation did anyone mention a number. This indicated clearly to me that they did not know what the number was.

"That's the wrong answer; the answer should be a number," I said to them. And we sat down to begin to figure it out. Together we quickly calculated that the interest cost of an unsold car was two dollars per day and that the average amount of time it sat on the lot was sixty days. Anyone could do the math to see that several hundred cars sitting idle for two months was quite a large expense.

One week later, at our next meeting, Wesley, the leader of the reconditioning unit said, "I told my guys about the two dollars per day interest cost, and they started making changes instantly. Where they used to check once a week to see if parts came in, they now check daily. If a part's come in, they move the car to the top of the list to be repaired, and we can get the cars out four or five days faster—that's ten dollars per car, and we're doing four hundred cars per week—that's a whole lot of money."

In front of the whole team, I said, "I'm going to come over and kiss you—that is the best thing I've heard all week." That evening, I thought to myself, *How amazing is it that in the space of one week, he not only got the concept but also had communicated it in his own words to his team—and that in one week, they had already made some progress.* What I didn't know was what was yet to come.

The following week, Wesley reported to the leadership team that his group had worked out how to calculate how long the cars were sitting in the shop, and that they had moved all the "older" ones to a dedicated area, which they nicknamed "Money Lane." They gave it that name because these cars were costing the company money, and they wanted to make sure there weren't many (or any) cars in Money Lane. Wesley and his team were figuring all of this out—themselves.

By week three, the team was able to get the inventory numbers I had originally asked for, and when we looked at the numbers, it was clear we had excess inventory. We now had a baseline number from which we could measure change. This determination led to a number of immediate decisions that the team could act on quickly. We also knew we had to "peel the onion" to get further information. It became obvious to everyone in the leadership group (looking at these numbers together) that, due to the compartmentalized organization and lack of information sharing, we had someone in acquisition buying cars based on what deals he could make, without fully considering how much money would be required to recondition the cars. The head of sales, who was responsible for selling the cars, had never provided input for buying or reconditioning cars. And the CFO, who had to fund the car purchases, could not plan his financing accurately because everything was so uncoordinated. So we created a car acquisition committee—consisting of four people—whose mission was to sort this out, develop a plan with metrics, and begin working on this issue.

Within the next few weeks, the data became much more precise. Car buyers were now given a shopping list of cars to acquire based on our current inventory—what cars were selling best, and which cars, from a quality perspective, needed fewer repairs and remained on the road longer. These four leaders meet briefly on a weekly basis to review and make decisions. Our inventory was reduced by ten days within the first six weeks, and this was only the beginning. After four months, the inventory was reduced by twenty-four days—an extraordinary accomplishment that Wesley and his team achieved themselves.

Wesley also apprised the team about several new initiatives; these had nothing to do with saving two dollars per day in interest but were about how his operation could improve its performance—managing parts suppliers more rigorously, reducing the number of outside body shops from fourteen to five, and others too numerous to mention. In other words, he got it.

There are a few significant takeaways from this hot button example. At the end of week two, Wesley reported out to his team about the two dollars per day interest cost, and he and his team immediately began to make decisions as a result. He never asked anyone for permission to take any of these actions; there were no meetings, no presentation decks, and very few email messages. And because he reported weekly to the management team about his progress, Wesley could see clearly how well received this information was by that team, which gave him further motivation to continue. And if there were questions or issues, they were resolved at the weekly meeting. His entire department became energized; they knew they were making a difference—even after only just a few weeks. Also, they were all having a lot more fun at their jobs because they were now doing more than repairing cars—they were changing the way they ran their department. In addition, the car acquisition committee began to break down the communication barriers that existed between their department and other departments, and develop a cross-functional team approach to buying, restoring, funding, and selling the cars.

All these results (which occurred after only six weeks)—and the many more that came later—started with the simple hot button of two dollars per day of interest cost per car. The outcome of this use of "focus" far exceeded my expectations. Hot buttons are like tiny sparks that can lead to igniting a whole team.

Of course every set of circumstances in any given business is totally unique. So how do you as a leader go about finding the hot buttons in your situation?

I spoke with Tom Hale, the founder and CEO of Backroads, the world's largest and most successful active travel company. Started in his garage thirty-seven years ago, it has grown dramatically and offers several hundred unique trips in forty-five countries around the world. Backroads' success is largely measured by an exceptionally high rate of repeat guests (on average about 80 percent become repeat and referral guests). "We focus on one key metric far and away more significantly than anything else," Hale told me, "which is our leader performance as measured by guests. Why? Most people, when you ask them about their trip, will say they loved it, but then will immediately go on for quite a while about how the leader was so great—and that, to me, is exemplary of why that is our key metric. There is pressure each and every day within the organization to move away from that key metric. If there is one hat I wear it's that we never move away from that key metric. Folks who work closely with the leaders often want to combine all sorts of other attributes that are important, with that key metric. And I can see that will water this down, to bring other issues into it, but we have managed to hold the line on that."[1]

There is no exact formula for finding hot buttons, but I find it works best to start by identifying the two or three (no more than that) critical drivers of the company. Ask each person in your leadership team to list on a piece of paper what they think the hot buttons are, and why. You will find that there will likely be overlap among the answers from the team members, but then there will also be some outliers. Often the outlier group will provide a better hot button because those leaders are being more imaginative. In addition to eliciting the team list, talk to other people—ask lots of questions, poke around, engage with folks both high and low. You will get additional ideas that you can bring back to the group. After you zero in on those that are the best, you have to be able to translate and quantify a simple metric for each of them (e.g., two dollars per day)—one that is very clear and digestible for everyone. Once you announce what the hot buttons are, everyone will be able to focus on the crucial core issues, not the peripheral matters that people often gravitate toward.

The beauty of these hot buttons, when chosen properly, is that they are very easy to communicate, and they are things that everyone in the company can grasp, regardless of their level of responsibility in the organization, their geographical location, etc. And hot buttons enable people—either on their own or working in loosely defined groups—to creatively problem solve, which by itself is very empowering to them and to everyone around them.

The Quick Win

It is very hard, some would say torturous, to get decisions made in large companies. Part of the reason for this that is the decision-making process is complicated, unwieldy, and generally risk averse. Most organizational structures have numerous layers just within the division or group responsible for selling products. In addition, the support functions—like finance, technology, marketing, etc.—essentially have parallel multilayered structures.

Some organization charts are so complicated that they can look like a New York City subway map. The senior leadership of the company must sign off on any important decision or any decision that involves substantial sums of money. Typically, if the recommendation originates at three or four levels below the CEO, it requires discussion and approval at each level before it can move up the chain of command.

Every organization has its own mechanism for making

decisions, but in larger organizations, decision making is quite time consuming, sometimes taking months. (Nobody sets it up to take this long; it happens for a variety of reasons, including the fact that meetings in general are undisciplined, as discussed in chapter 2.) Not all companies are the same, but the traditional approach involves extensive analysis, often very clinical analysis—usually put together by a team and presented in various meetings. PowerPoint presentations have become increasingly more sophisticated; the information is often presented with complex, carefully constructed charts, tables, and graphs—often with multiples of these elements on a single slide. Some of these slides can take over an hour to create. The intent of the analysis is to boil down the significant facts, issues, and concerns as they relate to the subject matter being reviewed. Typically, the information is historically based, and a majority of the presentation consists of financial estimates. This tends to reflect incremental thinking that, while less risky, may not sufficiently address the issue at hand. Unfortunately, much of the information represents a summarization of the current situation, rather than creative alternatives to really attack the problem.

After the extensive analysis has been done, a detailed plan is formulated and recommendations are made. While there is always a person who has to ultimately sign off on the plan, you first need to get feedback from a lot of people. In the lexicon of current business practice, you need to "socialize it."

What does this mean? Others have to be involved or feel as though they have some say in the plan. Often you need the support of other departments to even hope to get the plan through, and you need to find out if anyone has any issues with your proposal; after all, you are not operating in a vacuum. This "consensus seeking" could be done well and quickly. But most of the time these days it's not. There are often side and hidden agendas; various leaders may weigh in on issues that may be tangentially related but are not really on topic. Emotions can be involved; people have history with each other, both good and bad. It can be similar to the way Congress operates.

Reviews begin with your peers, the people on your level, and then move up to leaders on the next level. It's like an upward spiral that gets smaller at the top, and it's a slow and sometimes painful process. At the end of the process, the people who have to sign off get a finished product that is highly polished and sanitized. They never see what it took to get the recommendation into that form. No one ever gets to see how the sausage was made.

Most people believe (whether valid or invalid) that they can derail or veto the proposal, but very few have the power to sign off on it. If you are the sponsor of the proposal, you can feel almost like a piñata hanging from the ceiling—where everyone is going to step up one by one and give you a whack.

Sometimes, one of the consequences of this process is that the initiator waters down the request before he even presents it, to eliminate this piñata effect. The problem is that the new proposal hardly resembles the bold, imaginative, and impactful plan he envisioned at the beginning.

This is related to another detrimental and unconscious element of the standard decision-making process—what I call "settling for less." What this means is that instead of asking for a decision based on what would be great for the company, many managers are merely seeking to get something approved, and to maintain the approval of their superiors above all else. They may rationalize the dumbing down of their original idea by saying to themselves: *Well, at least we are sort of moving in the right direction.* Or they might be thinking: *What can we get senior management to sign off on without too much fuss, conflict, or many uncomfortable discussions?* They may really want the big win, the "ten," but they feel pretty sure they can't get it, so they don't ask for it. Instead they scale it back and go for a "five," which they believe they can sell. There is a strong element of fear of rejection in this system, which is obviously unproductive. It's telling people only what they want to hear, and it does not allow for real dialogue and change to occur. You ask for just enough to matter but not so much that it will raise too many issues and concerns.

Between the senior leaders not seeing the original proposal before it went through the "sausage maker"—the numerous rounds of meetings, discussions, and compromises—and the initiator fearing the rejection of his project, proposals are often substantially weaker and any original boldness or innovative idea may have been lost. The recommendation may be a step in the right direction, but it is not what the initiator wanted or conceived—or what the CEO was hoping for. The typical corporate structure can sometimes act like a giant sponge that unwittingly drains all the juice out of innovative impulses. In the end, no one really wins.

But there is a positive, productive way to "stay small" and still get large or ambitious projects approved, and it's not about compromising, or watering down anything. It's about simplifying what you ask for by separating what you need into separate components. I call this going for the "quick win."

For instance, I was sitting in on a review of a company that had four distinctly separate businesses; over the course of a two-hour meeting I saw presentations by each of the heads of these companies. One presentation by the head of a mid-level bicycle manufacturer in particular caught my attention. The division president was making a proposal to move into the higher-end price range of bikes—bikes featuring carbon frames as well as better quality brakes, gears, wheels, tires, and accessories.

Bill, the president, used very clear, simple slides and made the case that moving into the higher price range would generate substantially greater sales and profits and would enable the company to more aggressively compete. In fact, he showed that the company's previous few years of annual growth would essentially double from 6–7 percent to 12–13 percent. He also raised a number of insightful questions including: Were their existing customers, the ones who had been buying mid-level bikes from this company, likely to buy higher-end, more expensive bikes from them versus from the existing higher-end manufacturers? And if the answer was yes, how many of their customers would be likely to upgrade their purchase from a mid-level bike to a higher-end bike—meaning that the incremental sale value would only be the difference in price, not that of an additional bike sold? (If so, that needed to be taken into account in the annual growth estimate.) Also, were they sure they knew how to fabricate carbon bikes—a very different process from aluminum and steel bikes? How would their dealers react to them selling these higher-end bikes?

Bill told the group that he felt strongly this was a criti-cally important move for the company but that he was now only seeking permission for a first step: to invest up to $250,000 to better understand the market dynamics from the customer's perspective, including talking to existing and potential customers, meetings with dealers, understanding the logistics of fabricating carbon bikes, etc. The plan was to return in four months with these results, analysis, and recommendations to proceed—with the stated understand-ing that if all worked out, then a major financial request (in the range of $3 million) would be made for this expansion. If not, he'd move on to find another area for growth.

Bill went for the quick win. He knew how important it was to apprise the board about moving into more expensive bicycles, but he knew that serious analysis had to be done before he could present a compelling business case for such a large move. Bill was smart enough to begin with getting approval to proceed with just the first phase of the project. This gave him a good chance of ultimate success; not only was the senior leadership team now engaged in the project (because they found his growth plan immediately attrac-tive), but also their investing in the first step would make it easier to get final approval for what was a very substantial change—if the results from phase one were positive.

If you offer up the whole proposal all at once, and ask the powers that be for either a "yes" or "no," the answer is almost always going to be no. It's usually too weighty, too complicated; there is too much money involved, or too much perceived risk. It's always much easier for people to say no than yes. The way you mitigate all these objections is by breaking the project or recommendation into the bite-sized pieces. It's the first-things-first strategy that enables the quick win. If they only have to approve an initial move, then it's now easier for them to say yes (because they're not betting the ranch) and to say it quickly. It's like working with building blocks—and part of what you are building is consensus. And when you build consensus you create engagement. Let's face it; it's very hard to get people on board with change. But every time they give you a yes to a small section of your plan, they become more invested in a positive outcome of the whole effort. Therefore, it's much more effective and much faster to move toward your goal incrementally. Always remember, incremental does not mean slow; neither does it imply a weakening of the proposal. Going for a quick win is not the same as settling for less, or reducing your ask. On the contrary, by moving forward piece by logical piece, you will probably succeed more quickly in whatever your comprehensive plan is, and you are also more likely to keep that plan undiluted.

There is a notion prevalent in business that aiming big—trying to do it all, taking one giant leap in a single bound—is a sign of a true leader. But often, smaller is better. In many cases you need a wide lens on your inner camera—to see the big picture, look outside your own conference room, and then zoom in on the target. But there is also great value in narrowing your focus. A small amount of push in the right direction can start an avalanche of change.

CHAPTER FIVE

UNLEASHING YOUR TEAM: ENGAGING YOUR EMPLOYEES

"People are definitely a company's greatest asset. It doesn't
make any difference whether the product is cars or cosmetics.
A company is only as good as the people it keeps."

—Mary Kay Ash

By far the biggest secret weapon you have—or that any
company has—is your own employees. Your employees are
your most valuable assets, but you have to be proactive to
find and unleash the hidden power inherent in your organization. To begin this process, you need to get the lay of the
land—to understand the perspectives of both your leaders
and employees, and what their relationship is to each other.

First, I strongly believe that most employees are good
people who want to do a good job. Having spent over
thirty-five years working in and leading companies as well
as advising them, I think I have developed a pretty accurate
sense of the dynamics at play in organizations. Employees spend more time at work than anywhere else in their
twenty-four-hour day, and they would like to feel productive and satisfied, and hopefully look forward to coming

back tomorrow. They are looking for someone to engage with them, to make their job as interesting and meaningful as possible and to allow them to contribute and grow—in addition to earning a salary (which is the primary reason it is called work and not vacation).

Second, it is also important to understand and appreciate that there is no real pact or bargain today between employees and employers; they each serve at the whim of the other. If the employee finds a better job, he's gone. If the company decides to restructure the organization, then twenty (or two hundred) folks are let go. This is quite a different framework from the "I do a good job, have a career with the company, and stay until retirement" ideology that typified American business after World War II. While this fundamental concept no longer exists, employers are still looking for great employees to fully dedicate themselves to the company, and employees are looking for organizations that will appreciate their skills, effort, and talent. Employees witness companies sending jobs offshore, outsourcing entire departments, reducing hours to avoid providing health-care benefits, and implementing other cost measures designed to improve profitability. From the employers' vantage point, employees are more concerned about themselves than their work, want to earn more than they deserve, and will leave at a moment's notice if another better position comes along.

Third, it is a safe bet that most of your employees are not very engaged (regardless of their level in the company)—or at least not as engaged as they could be. Because of things that you or others may have done and said in the past, many of your employees could well believe that you think of them merely as a cost—in much the same way that you view office space, computers, and trucks. In other words, all other things being equal, you should assume the situation is broken. This idea is counterintuitive to most leaders; as a rule we don't want to go looking for trouble and prefer to take the position that unless we see obvious problems, everything is fine. However, just because you don't see smoke pouring out of the second-story windows doesn't mean there's not a fire in the basement. Your best course of action is to start with the notion that there is a lot of work to be done. It is incumbent on you, as the leader— and your leadership team—to engage your people.

There are several ways to begin to unleash the power of your team, but it begins with looking at things with fresh eyes, and committing to engaging. Engagement needs to start at the top, and it will flow downward throughout the organization, like water; after all, water cannot flow up. Each of the Five Principles of Engagement must be employed from the top down, and connecting is one of these. Senior leaders need to create an atmosphere of involvement and trust along with designing processes that encourage two-way communication. Leaders connect by interacting authentically with employees, not by dictating to them. As a leader, you need to become a bit more human—by not being afraid to show emotions, by revealing your true personality, and by stepping out of the stereotypical role of "boss." All of us have been inculcated not to do this—we are trained not to reveal our true selves in the business world; so for many leaders, this will not come naturally.

I have always considered myself lucky that I truly enjoy talking to people—everyone, everywhere, and all the time. I find it very motivating and interesting to see how other people think, whether I'm waiting in line to get a coffee or

I am sitting next to someone on an airplane or in the company cafeteria. However, you don't have to be born gregarious; engaging with people is something you can train yourself to do.

Principles versus Rules

Rules become the rails that the company train rides on. Most large organizations have rules—in some cases hundreds or thousands of them. They accumulate over the course of years and each is created for a very specific reason at the time; that is, somewhere along the line a new problem develops or an issue arises, and in fixing the problem, someone creates a new rule. Of course, the purpose of rules is to make sure there are repeatable, reliable processes and no mistakes—a noble goal. Rules are often a major barrier to engagement, and there can be unintended consequences of rules. Rules force employees to think in a binary way: they either authorize an MRI procedure or decide it's not warranted; allow the passenger to board the plane now, or make her wait; authorize a refund, or tell the customer why it will not happen; and so on.

The problem is that while rules are black and white, the real world is gray. Employees, coworkers, customers, and leaders are all operating in the "gray" world, not within the sterile, inflexible dimension of rules. Not surprisingly, many leaders who favor the traditional command-and-control business culture find it difficult to imagine a world with fewer rules; to them, fewer rules mean a loss of control. Yet as the world moves faster and information is omnipresent, rules—which tend to be static—very often cannot keep up with the demands of the market and the needs of your customers. The consequence of rigid rules is that they often place well-intentioned employees (and in turn customers) in an unnecessary conflict, simply because they are required to adhere to those rules—some of which may have been instituted ten years ago.

Principles are different from rules. They speak to values, to what is really important in a given situation. They provide structure, guidelines, and parameters. They define the boundaries relating to what is permissible and what is not, but they also provide leeway, so that individual judgment can be used in the moment—allowing for the best possible outcome given a specific set of circumstances. Principles also require a level of trust between leaders and employees. They say: "We've trained you, given you all the necessary tools, and explained what's important—and we expect you to operate within this framework and use your best judgment." That, in and of itself, requires a leader to relinquish some control—something that many leaders are not comfortable doing. And the employee—once he is given the leeway—has the responsibility to not behave like a robot; he needs to think, assess, act, and make a decision that works for both the company and the customer.

Most of us recognize and appreciate when people are acting according to principles rather than strict rules. For instance, last year I took a trip to Asia and about a week before I was scheduled to leave I was told that I needed to take a CAT scan test before I went. The scheduling desk gave me a Saturday morning appointment, and I was grateful they could accommodate me on such short notice. However, because they had rushed to fit me in, they missed the note on my chart that I am allergic to iodine. Being allergic to iodine, I needed to be premedicated in order to safely take the test (which they forgot to tell me). I was sent home and told to contact my doctor so that he could prescribe the medication that would allow me to proceed with the test. Unfortunately, they would not let me reschedule the test until twenty-four hours after I had taken the medication, and it seemed unlikely I would be able to schedule it before my departure, putting my trip at risk. Luckily the supervisor, Mabel, stepped in and said to me, "I will take care of this for you—here is my personal phone number. You call me after you've taken the pills, and I will get you in ASAP. I will personally make sure that you can have this properly checked out so you can go and enjoy your trip."

Mabel squeezed me in on Tuesday. While I was walking into the test room, a person in the waiting room was complaining that her appointment was delayed (I assume because of me), but Mabel ignored her. She instinctually knew to make an exception—because I was about to leave the country for three weeks and really needed this test— and she probably felt comfortable enough that her seniors would support her decision if it were questioned. This type of interaction creates a lasting bond between a customer and a company when done right. Mabel operated on the principle of taking care of a patient rather than blindly following the rules.

Large organizations have the most rules, both the written or "official" ones and the ones that inexplicably come into existence all on their own. When I ask people about why they are following what appears to be a strange rule, most of the time no one can explain why the rule exists or what condition occurred to initiate the rule. Sometimes people laugh at the absurdity of some of these rules, but it actually isn't funny, and it's also not good business.

Here is a good example of how an arbitrary rule can get started. A call center company, tracking its results very carefully, determined that its agents were staying on a call with customers for an average of three and a half minutes, which they thought was way too long. Rather than determine why this was happening, the top brass instructed managers to drive down the time each agent was on a call. One manager got so excited by this, he proudly told his leadership team that his calls averaged less than one minute! Of course, that manager's customers had to call the company back because their problem was not properly addressed, which made them increasingly unhappy.

The cumulative effect of having rigid rules is similar to what would happen if the pilot and the brakeman on a bobsled team switched positions. Watching a bobsled race always amazes me, because so much happens within a very short period of time, in a highly organized way. Basically, four big guys all jump into an aerodynamically designed sled to go down this icy track on a giant mountain. The front guy (the pilot) jumps in first and steers. The next two guys (called pushers because their power is critical in getting a good start) jump in sequentially after the pilot and serve to balance the sled through numerous and treacherous turns. The last guy who jumps into the sled is the brakeman. His job is to modulate their speed so that they can go as fast as possible without flying off the track. With the sled reaching speeds of eighty miles an hour, the team is all about flexibility and finesse—principles, not rules. All four riders need to be fully in sync—reacting to one another and making instantaneous decisions with their body movements. Everyone has a job on the sled; and to win the race, everyone needs to operate at peak performance.

In many companies, following the rules is a little like putting the brakeman in the front of the sled, instead of the pilot. The brakeman is only interested in not crashing; after all, that's his job. Speed is not as important. And so what happens in these companies is that there is no momentum, no energy, no action—just brakes.

Simply put, the problem with rules is they are fixed and cannot cover every situation. Circumstances change; what might have been a great rule eight years ago might be ridiculous today. Management prefers predictability and conformance (both are related to control). They don't want people to take initiative for fear they might do something wrong. Theoretically, rules are supposed to limit the damage that can be done. But they also limit the good that can be done. How might employees and customers interact if employees were allowed to think and exercise their own judgment within some basic parameters?

Because they utilize an open system, principles afford employees the latitude to do what they think is right. They provide room to move, room to make the sale. Principles require more thought to create than rules; however, if you train employees well, using a structure of principles to follow, the upside is huge for the owner. Moreover, the employees will feel more empowered, have more fun, and in some cases may make more money for themselves as well.

Here is a really good example to demonstrate this point. When I ran the Sears credit card business, we used to get millions of customer service calls each year. Many of these calls were from customers disputing charges that appeared on their monthly billing statements. In some cases, our agents were able to resolve the question immediately, while in other cases, further research was required. I had seen a report that a substantial percentage of these cases requiring research were for amounts under fifty dollars, and I wondered what our fully loaded cost was to investigate these questions. The analysis showed that it cost us about thirty-five dollars per inquiry, which I felt was pretty expensive for us. Because we were processing enormous volumes of these transactions, I suggested to my team that going forward, if the dispute was for twenty-five dollars or less, we would offer a credit to the customer on the spot and eliminate the entire research process—making the customer happy and saving us ten dollars per inquiry. Seems simple, right?

But a funny thing happened. Programmed by years of rules and procedures, employees either thought we were giving away something to customers they did not deserve, or felt strongly we should not institute this policy because customers would invariably "take advantage of us." How and when did this thought process begin? Why did they assume our customers would suddenly devise a plan to rip us off? Our employees had been following the rules for so long that breaking them actually made them suspicious of their customers. We implemented the change, made our customers very happy, and actually made more money in this department. I firmly believe that in an organization that had been led with principles instead of rules, the employees would not have reacted this way and might well have come up with the idea themselves.

Most companies already have everything they need to do it right; they just don't realize it. The key is to inspire, not to command—and to treat employees like adults. If they don't do well, train them better or replace them, but don't treat them like children. Allow them the space to show initiative.

HERE ARE A FEW
APPROACHES I USE THAT WORK WELL:

- Don't give orders to your leaders. Make sure they are totally informed about what is going on and ask them questions about how they plan to address particular issues. Engage with them rather than telling them, especially your leaders at the higher levels. After all, these are people to whom you've entrusted tremendous responsibility; so let them figure out how do their jobs.

- Make sure employees know the rules are going to be changing and that many rules will be replaced with principles—but that it is going to happen over time. This change must be gradual, because you do not want to cause an earthquake within your operation.

- Treat each situation you encounter as an opportunity to change a rule into a principle. This "bite-sized" approach limits your risk, and it also makes it easier for employees to begin to understand that change is on the way, and it's good.

- After you have been working on this for a few months, ask your middle- and lower-level leaders to identify some rules that can be changed—and ask them how they would change those rules into principles. You will be amazed at how quickly they will grasp these concepts and help you lead the charge.

The Importance of Challenging the Status Quo

During the writing of this book, a shocking story came out about Volkswagen. It was discovered that eleven million diesel vehicles sold in the United States and Europe contained a so-called software-enabled "defeat device," which effectively lowered vehicle emissions for regulatory testing purposes. Basically it was a technique to deceive the regulatory agencies and their customers, by falsely lowering the levels of pollutants that were actually being emitted, but only during emissions tests. The United States Environmental Protection Agency issued a notice on September 18, 2015, that the car marker had violated the Clean Air Act.[1]

Two days later, VW admitted the deception.[2] The stock dropped 20 percent and declined another 17 percent the next day. On September 23, CEO Martin Winterkorn resigned[3] (which was followed by another six executives resigning in the ensuing days). Four weeks after the initial scandal broke, Volkswagen, for the first time in its history, offered a thirty-day amnesty program to all employees (excluding management) if they would come forward and tell what they knew about how this happened.[4] Obviously this investigation came way too late. The crisis continued to unfold for many months—and will continue for years to come—with potential civil and criminal lawsuits, customers wondering what will happen to their cars, and leaders and employees wondering what the next moves will be.

Like so many people, I could not help wondering how this could have happened to one of the largest and most respected global automakers. What level of disconnect within Volkswagen could have caused such an outcome? What kind of management processes allowed this to occur? What caused employees and leaders to be silent when they knew this was wrong? Why hadn't the board of directors been aware of this situation so they could proactively deal with it?

It is pure speculation of course, and it is unclear exactly who was culpable, but I have seen similar crisis-level situations before, and here is a plausible scenario.

The company and its CEO announced ten years ago that they would be launching a new line of diesel cars that would be extremely fuel efficient, green, and would perform better than their current models. Some factions within VW intended to purchase Mercedes' BlueTEC system for reducing pollution, but other factions rejected that and preferred to develop their own system.[5] A substantial amount—perhaps billions of euros—would be invested to develop the technology and manufacturing facilities built to produce these cars.

Along the way, various delays occurred in developing the new technology, but the launch date was never revised because the launch was "carved in stone." Downstream leaders were afraid to tell their bosses there were issues. (VW leadership has been well known for a command-and-control style "on steroids.") So some of the engineers developed a software program, the sole purpose of which was to allow the car to falsely pass the test for the government regulatory certification. This meant the cars that were sold were neither in compliance with the law nor did they have the gas mileage performance that had been marketed to customers. I can't help thinking that the CEO and/or the senior leadership must have fostered an atmosphere of fear that helped produce this disaster—that some or many employees were afraid to tell those at the top about the development of the software—or, if senior people did know, that employees were afraid to tell them it was a bad idea. Or—and this is the crux of it—that too few employees said, "Wait—what are we doing here? Why are we doing this? We need to pull the fire alarm lever!"

It will take years for Volkswagen to dig itself out of this situation—a situation that could have been entirely prevented if leaders had felt comfortable enough to raise their hands and say there was a problem. A *New York*

Times article in December 2015 reported that a former VW employee, Mr. Arndt Ellinghorst, who is now an automotive industry analyst at an investment advisory firm, decided not to stay at Volkswagen, partly due to its management style. "VW had this special culture," he said. "It was like North Korea without labor camps," he added, quoting a famous description of the company published in *Der Spiegel* magazine. "You have to obey."[6]

Of course this is an extreme example. There are many different degrees of this kind of sheeplike, nonquestioning behavior. Not all of them result in real harm to the corporation, as in the Volkswagen instance. When I spoke with Andrew Florance of CoStar, he told me another kind of story that illustrates how important it is to have engaged employees—ones who question what they are doing—and what can happen if they don't.

"There was one company we acquired that gave an annual customer event, a dinner," Florance said, "where they would have their biggest customers come together. So we're having this dinner, and the person responsible for running the conference, comes up to me and says 'We have an emergency.'

"'What is it?' I asked.

"'Well, I made it clear that the hotel was not supposed to serve key lime pie,' she says, 'and the waiters are putting key lime pie down.'

"So I assume someone is allergic to key lime pie, but she's not sure who. And I say 'So what are you going to do?'

"She says, 'I'm going to tell the waiters to start pulling it up right away.'

"So I say, 'Okay. As long as you do that before this guy takes the first bite.'

"So she dashes off, and the waiters start pulling pie. But I'm thinking to myself, *But wouldn't this guy look at the key lime pie and know it was key lime pie? He's like, fifty years old, couldn't he figure this out? What are we talking about here?*

"I went over to her and said, 'Wait a minute, is someone allergic to it?' And she answered, 'No no, Judy B_____ said she hates key lime pie and never wants key lime pie served at the conference.'

"So as I'm watching the waiters running around taking pie off people's tables, I say to her, 'Judy left the company ten years ago, she died five years ago—she's not eating the pie!'"[7]

You see it again and again: Something got set in motion by someone who had the ability to understand what's happening, and why it's happening, and then it goes into perpetual motion—it becomes a rule without the people executing it questioning why it happens or whether it made any sense for it to happen in the first place. If the conference woman had been engaged, operating with fresh eyes, she would not have blindly followed the "no key lime pie" rule for ten years. There would have been some kind of discussion (i.e., why is key lime pie not a good dessert to serve at the conference?). Obviously, the banning of a dessert is of minor consequence, but what happened at Volkswagen was anything but minor. When people don't question rules or policies, there can be serious and negative results.

There is always an answer to why something happens; people typically don't act out of randomness. Something caused an action or rule to be set in motion, but so often it is blindly accepted and followed. It gets locked in, and it can do a lot of damage when it is not challenged.

SHAKING THINGS UP

One way to get your employees to engage is to do something unusual to get them to become more aware of what they are doing and how it affects the organization as a whole. (Fresh eyes are not always so easy to manifest; sometimes people need help). I was reminded of this when I spoke with Claes Landberg, who is general manager of YOTEL in New York City and someone with over twenty years of management experience. YOTEL is a fairly new hotel concept that provides a cool, affordable luxury hotel experience. He was telling me about how he gets a team energized, how to get the individual members of the team to engage or reengage—involving them, and letting them have a say.

"I will never forget this. I was just at the beginning of my career, and I was sitting having lunch in the little restaurant I was managing in Stockholm. My dishwasher was talking about what a failure he was in life, because he was only a dishwasher. And that was tough for me, hearing him talk like that, you know, someone that works for you. It was a new environment for me; I think I was nineteen or something like that at the time. It kept bothering me, eating away at me. I couldn't think about anything else the whole night. So the next day I decided to do an experiment. It was an experiment that I think worked very well, even though I would do it very differently today.

"I decided to have him not do the dishes for this lunch. Now, this was a seventy-seat restaurant; we did about 250–300 covers per lunch, with 202 plates available. So if no one washes the dishes, guess what's happens? So, after breakfast service, I told the dishwasher, 'Just sit here. I don't want you to touch the dishes for the entire lunch service.' He looked at me like I had three heads, but he did what I said.

"And then we start lunch, the restaurant fills up very quickly, the second seating starts, the pile of clean plates keeps going down, and finally the last ten clean plates are taken out of the kitchen, and I hear the chef and everybody start yelling 'Hey I need plates, I need plates!'

"And then I just take everybody into the kitchen, and I say to them, 'Okay everybody stop what you are doing.'

"'I'm very sorry to say but we are closing down the restaurant. Unfortunately, we cannot stay open because we don't have plates to serve our guests. What does that mean? That means that none of you have jobs anymore. You don't have a paycheck to put food on the table for your families. I'm sorry that Christmas is going to be a little bit difficult for you this year.'

"And everyone starts saying, 'What are you talking about?' And at that point I turn to the dishwasher, and I tell him, 'This is how important you are. Everyone in this room—and their families—depend on you doing your job and doing it very well.'

"Of course," Landberg continued, "this was a drastic way to prove a point, but I've never seen anyone wash the dishes the way he did after that. Later my crew asked me, 'Why didn't you let us in on the deal? You scared the s**t out of us.' But of course that would have lessened the impact. And really after that we always had that openness— we worked together. Yes, we were a small team. But we understood everything one of us did affected everyone."[8]

I used a "shaking things up" method of my own on one occasion, and while we got really good results, I must admit it was quite a challenge to implement. A medium-sized company I had invested in (and was on the board of) was performing well, though not as well as we believed they were capable of. After spending a few days at an off-site meeting with the CEO and the reasonably strong leadership team, I came up with the idea that they would all switch jobs with one another for one week. That way all of them could approach their new roles with fresh eyes, and might be able to see more clearly what else could be done in that role.

After lots of discussion, they agreed to do this—although of course we had to set ground rules, agree on protocols, etc. What happened was that, after we navigated all the interpersonal roadblocks (people not wanting to insult each other by pointing out things that hadn't been done right in the past, etc.), many good suggestions were made that were developed and implemented into long-term projects. And all the leaders gained a better sense of the issues their colleagues were facing, which led to a higher level of teamwork going forward. Not only does this method engender company-wide fresh eyes, it also serves to connect leaders to each other in a new way.

GETTING PEOPLE TO ASK QUESTIONS

The truth is that most people are afraid to ask questions—whether from years of conditioning within a company or plain old human nature. Whatever natural curiosity they had as children tends to get discouraged in most large organizations. Leaders assume following the status quo is the right way to go and are not interested in trying to challenge anything, especially if it seems on the surface to be going along just fine. And the lower-level employees just try to do what's asked of them and stay out of trouble—believing that people who ask questions may be sticking their neck out.

Obviously, getting people to start asking questions— getting them to use fresh eyes and then act on that new perspective—requires effort and energy. It means changing what may have been part of a process for years. Change is very hard. It actually means choosing the path of resistance, instead of the path of least resistance. But when people get into the habit and know they won't get their heads chopped off for asking questions, that in fact their questions will be welcomed, everything gets better.

The best way to teach is by example. Buddha and every other great leader throughout history taught by showing or doing, not by telling. When your people see you, the leader, asking questions (i.e., questions about how and why things are done, not questions regarding people's individual intentions and/or productivity), they will begin to feel comfortable answering your questions, and they will start asking similar questions with their folks. And those folks, in turn, will start to realize that challenging things and offering information about what is really going on in their department is something that is encouraged. When you are willing to admit in front of everybody that you don't know a particular answer, and you are the boss, then that makes others understand that they also can admit they don't know. This enables free flowing information, which is essential to the health and productivity of your organization.

This sounds pretty simple doesn't it? So why does this reticence, this reluctance to ask questions, occur so often? Why is it so hard for leaders to know what's going on at the lower levels of their companies? The main reason is that leaders are fundamentally not interacting well with their employees.

Obviously most leaders don't promote a closed-door

policy or a bad environment. They just don't actively promote the opposite. But the absence of a positive message is still a message, just as making no decision is actually making an important decision—a decision to do nothing. The process of questioning is actually hard—and it is a *process*. There are no simple approaches here to reset what has been years in the making.

When I interviewed Denis Picard, a managing director who specializes in technology and operations with Alvarez & Marsal's Business Performance Improvement in New York, he told me a story that illustrates what can happen when people don't ask questions.

"We had a client in Boston," said Picard, "a communications technology manufacturer, rapidly growing, who needed to put in a new ERP [enterprise resource planning] system. As I'm sure you know, ERP systems have a high risk of failure, and if you don't have senior management support you cannot succeed.

"This Boston client had picked a system, configured the system, converted the data, and they were ready to go. Then the CFO, who is a friend of mine, called me and asked me if I would come take a look. He said they were supposed to go live, but he wasn't feeling good about what was happening.

"So I spent some time looking into it and found out that the implementation has stalled. They were supposed to go live maybe in a month or two, but things were at a standstill. I had a conversation with the CIO, who was the project leader, and I asked him what the problem was.

"'We lack senior management support,' he told me. 'Wow,' I said. 'That sounds pretty serious. Why do you say that?' 'Because the CFO won't help us,' was his answer. And

I thought, That's interesting because the CFO was the one who asked me to check into this. What's he doing wrong?

"So we kept talking about this," said Picard, "and it turns out they couldn't complete the final test and go live unless they bought a special printer—because they had to do some kind of labels that go on circuit boards or something like that—but in any case it was a very special printer, and it was going to cost $12,000."

When I asked Picard what the CFO had said when the CIO informed him of this, he told me the CIO had hesitated and then replied, "Well we haven't really asked him."

"Why not?" Picard had wanted to know. "Why wouldn't you have asked him?"

"He's going to say no," the CIO said. "Because it's very expensive. I can't ask him; it would be really bad for my career."

Picard went to the CFO to report back and told him, tongue in cheek, "Well, I found out that you are the problem."

The CFO looked at him kind of quizzically and said, "What are you talking about?"

"My understanding," said Picard, "is that you will not approve a $12,000 printer that you don't know anything about, and that's going to cause the project to be delayed."[9] The CFO was nonplussed. Absurdly enough, the project was costing about $5 million, and a $12,000 printer was holding it hostage. Of course in the end they bought the printer and finished the project.

If you engage your employees, they will not be afraid to come to you and tell you what is really happening. Their natural curiosity will come back, and they will start questioning things. However, this is a process that requires constant fine-tuning. For instance, at one company where I am involved, I offered up the idea of launching a company newsletter, so everyone would feel more connected. They liked the idea, and a small team put together the first newsletter, which was great and professionally done. Then, a couple of weeks later in a meeting, I asked everyone what their folks thought about the newsletter, and someone piped up with, "Well, the guys in our department didn't get mentioned, so they are pissed off." So I told him to go back and tell the team in that department to show everyone what they were made of and try to win the contest to name the newsletter. The point is, suggesting the newsletter was only step one; I asked what people thought about it, which provoked a conversation, concern, and subsequent action. It never stops, and the more everyone speaks up, the better it is.

When Alan Mulally was recruited from Boeing to become the CEO of Ford Motor Company, the company was experiencing serious financial difficulties—and this was prior to the recession. Historically, Ford had been a very siloed, highly bureaucratized organization that was still heavily controlled by the heirs of Henry Ford. Business reviews were totally predictable and no one ever discussed bad news. All presentations were positive—but if everything was going so well why was the company in trouble?

At review sessions, Mulally kept asking his leaders to identify and highlight issues in their presentations with red (problems), yellow (caution), and green (good)—yet all the information was coded as either green or yellow. Finally at one meeting, an executive named Mark Fields shocked everyone by presenting a chart with a red box, indicating a technical problem with the Ford Edge—a problem that would result in an expensive delay. Reportedly, Mulally started clapping; he thanked Fields for raising the issue and then suggested how a few of the leaders in that meeting could assist.[10] In *Fortune* magazine, Mulally is quoted as saying "Communicate, communicate, communicate. Everyone has to know the plan, its status, and areas that need special attention."[11] Mulally did a great job reinvigorating Ford, without requiring federal government assistance from the TARP program or taking the company through the bankruptcy process as did General Motors and Chrysler. Last year, Mark Fields was named CEO of Ford, and I do not think it was an accident that someone like him was able to move into that role.

Getting your employees to ask questions starts with you letting your hair down. Start a dialog. Begin with engagement.

Of course, as I said in chapter 3, there are some people who are born introverts; interacting with people does not come easily to them. They are afraid of saying the wrong thing, of offending someone, of looking stupid if they don't know the answer to something. There are many different methods to encourage people to open up so you can get to the nitty-gritty of what's going on. But you can't do this superficially. If you are not truly engaged in this process, then it will not work. So how do you begin to practice this? If this does not come naturally to you, here's a list of things you might do. Even if you are someone who is not comfortable talking to lots of people and asking questions, choose one or two that suit you the best, ones that feel the most natural to you. And then just start engaging.

HERE ARE SOME EASY
AND PAINLESS WAYS TO BEGIN:

- Have a conversation with your assistant and ask him how things are going. If you have never really done this before, with someone you know, you will find out immediately that there are things he will tell you that you never knew—and will want to know.

- Ask your assistant if he can suggest a few individuals he thinks would be willing to be open with you. Then you can reach out to them and arrange to meet with them individually. These chats do not have to be more than fifteen or twenty minutes.

- Make yourself talk to one new person every day—no matter who it is. Choose someone you would not normally talk to. At the end of the week, ask yourself, "Did I do this? Did I engage with someone new?" Believe it or not this will be fun, and you will almost always learn something that is beneficial. Once you realize it's not a waste of time, you will naturally do more of it. Like the Hot Button principle, starting small is the way you begin anything new, whether it's learning the saxophone, training for a marathon, or getting your people to ask questions.

- Convene a small group of employees into a conference room in their department (not your conference room) and say something like this: "I just wanted to come down and visit with you to see how you are all doing. I'd like to hear from you about what's working in your department, what's not—where you think we can improve, etc. I will probably take some notes to make sure I can address the items you bring up." Go around the table and ask them to tell you their name and what their job is. Usually before people finish introducing themselves, someone will make a comment that sparks a conversation among the group members, and we're off to the races. Before you know it, an hour is up and you have pages of notes.

Connecting Through Storytelling

It's no secret that one of the most effective ways to communicate an idea to people is through stories. People have been doing this since the beginning of time. Storytelling is one of the easiest methods of connecting to another human being. You can get your point across in a way that they can relate to and remember. The most successful people are often excellent storytellers.

In his book *Tell to Win*, Peter Guber—chairman and CEO of Mandalay Entertainment and producer of movies such as *Batman, The Witches of Eastwick*, and *Flashdance*—talks about the incredible power of storytelling. He took a group of ten friends on a five-day serious rafting trip on the Colorado River in the Grand Canyon. These friends were all-stars in their respective fields, and were all supremely confident individuals. For the first couple of days, they were all horsing around, and Guber knew they were not taking the very real danger in front of them seriously enough. So far they had all been pretty much ignoring the instructions of the expedition guides, and he felt if they didn't start taking things seriously, there was a real danger someone could die.

As they came ashore the third day, they could hear what sounded like a train roaring by. But of course it was not a train but the "class 10 rapid"[12] that was just around the bend. Guber took the group up the canyon to look at the thirty-seven-foot drop—the waterfall they were going to go over the next day. That made everyone nervous enough to be receptive to one of Peter Guber's stories. It was a Joseph Campbell–type tale that took place in ancient Egypt, and was about a hunting party traveling on the Nile. The story was about a king, a crocodile spirit, and learning to respect the perils of crossing the river. Every one of the previously joking members of the rafting group paid rapt attention during the telling of the tale. After hearing the story, they got it: It was time to stop messing around. They needed to concentrate on navigating the river. And they all listened to his rules about rafting much more than if he hadn't told the story.

This technique is an essential one if you want to be an effective leader. If I just give you the instructions without the story, even very simple instructions, they often go in one ear and out the other. But wrapped in the import of a vivid narrative, it becomes an impactful message. You've got to draw people in when you want to get your point across. Our mothers and fathers told us stories when we were kids (I can still remember many of those stories). Most of us still respond to stories more than any other kind of communication.

When I was at Citibank, I attended a four-day training seminar. These were backbreaking meetings, one after another; and toward the end of the seminar our brains were ready to explode. On the next to the last day, they said to us, "We're going to have a project for you to work on after dinner." So we had dinner, and of course everyone drank wine during dinner so that by the end of it some people were already drunk. Everyone else was just fried from the meetings. And then the leaders broke us up into groups of ten people each and gave each of us one piece of paper, printed double-sided. On it was a story that I recall pretty vividly.

You are on the plane, going cross-country, and something happens en route, and you wind up flying across Northern Canada. The plane crashes, and a lot of passengers die in the crash. You are the ten people who have survived. Included on the sheet was a very short list of items that are available to you. No one has proper clothing for the Arctic. There is no food left on the plane because it had gone past the dinner service. You are left with a compass, a can opener, a broken mirror, a shoehorn, and other random items like that. There are no communications or emergency radio available, you are in the middle of nowhere, and you don't know where you are; there is no map. Everything, all the instrumentation in the plane is dead, no battery or anything.

Together the team had to make a decision—and there was only one decision to make: Do we wait for help to come, or do we leave and look for help? The only rule was that the team decision had to be unanimous. We started the exercise at 10 p.m. And we went at it until 4 a.m. In the beginning of the process, everyone was making jokes and goofing around, but as the time wore on, our discussions got more serious, and heated.

Among our ten-person group, factions evolved; four different approaches were taking form, but we were clearly spinning our wheels. Ultimately I said, "Why don't we see which of us knows anything about this subject? (I grew up in the Bronx and don't know anything about the Arctic or camping.) I asked the group, "Does anyone know about navigation or extreme cold?" Several people started talking about their own experiences: how you prevent hypothermia, etc. After several hours we, as a group, decided we could go into the fuselage of the plane and block off the holes damaged in the crash, use the luggage to keep out the wind and animals, use a mirror to melt snow so we could make water, etc.

Ultimately, we decided to wait for help. There were ten teams; seven decided to go, three decided to wait. It turned out the correct answer for this exercise was to wait, the idea being that airline and rescue services knew the plane was down, and they would ping the transponder and eventually find it. If you left, you would probably die, either from animal attacks, by freezing to death, or whatever.

So what was the purpose of this story, this exercise? Because the decision needed to be unanimous, it was about us working together as a team: Someone had to lead, someone had to step up. Someone else had to adjudicate. It was storytelling used as team practice, and it was quite effective.

I use stories all the time to motivate people. For example this one: In 1978, I was twenty-seven years old, and I got promoted to CFO of a business for Citicorp. It was a big leap for me at the time, and I moved to Los Angeles for the job. We bought a company that had to be carved out of a larger company, and we had one year to accomplish this. And it didn't go well. In fact, it was a disaster. Everything was bad. And the senior vice president who oversaw this transaction was a tough Irishman we'll call O'Malley. He was a very tough guy, and as our performance deteriorated, he got increasingly tougher.

O'Malley created a form, and he said to me, "I want you to fill out this form every day and fax it to me." On the form were all the key indicators of the business. He didn't explain it to me. He just told me, "Fill it out and send it to me." All of us in the company were busy bailing water. Everything was broken, and we were doing everything possible trying to fix it. No one even had time to sleep. We didn't know what the hell we were doing. I would give this form to the leadership team and say,

"We've got to fill this out so I can give this to O'Malley first thing in the morning."

So my team would consolidate all the numbers, and then my secretary would fax the form to his secretary. O'Malley would call me every morning at eleven o'clock, and he would start asking me questions about the information on the form I had just sent him. I didn't know the answer to any of these questions because I hadn't filled it out. A lot of the information was incorrect, and the people who filled it out didn't give a damn. So, he would curse at me. He would say, "You don't know anything!" After a few days of this, I realized this was stupid. So I called everyone into the conference room and said, "Listen guys, let me explain what happens. Every day at eleven o'clock I get my ass kicked by O'Malley because I can't answer his questions about our form. The numbers are not accurate. So I want you guys to be more careful completing this form, and we are going to meet at 4 p.m. every day before I submit the form to him. I'm going to ask you the same kinds of questions that O'Malley asks me. You need to understand your information and explain it to me, so I will have the answers by the time he calls me at eleven the next day."

And then I said to them, "If you don't do this, you're going to be the ones on the phone with O'Malley at eleven o'clock, and trust me you don't want that to happen." (They looked at me in terror, because from what I told them, they knew O'Malley was a person you did not want to be on the wrong side of). This caused them to do lots of work.

So guess what? Little by little the numbers became more accurate, and we started to figure everything out. The conversations between O'Malley and me started to get better. And then one day he didn't call. I figured he was on vacation, or sick . . . he didn't call the next day or the next day. So finally I called him.

I said, "O'Malley, why haven't you been calling? I miss you."

He said, "I don't need to."

I said, "Why not?"

"I know you are all over it," he said to me.

I told this entire story to the president of a company I was working with at the time of writing this book, who had a similar situation. "You have to be O'Malley," I said. "You have to meet with them every day at 9 a.m., review this daily KPI [key performance indicator] report, and not stop asking questions until they understand that you are serious about addressing these problems and they also understand how to fix them. And then you can stop going over there."

"You're O'Malley," I reiterated at the end.

"I got it," he said.

I tell the O'Malley story whenever I come across a leader who is not pushing his people hard enough. It works every time.

There is an old Native American saying: "Tell me a fact, and I'll learn it. Tell me a truth, and I'll believe. But tell me a story, and it will live in my heart forever." There is really no teaching tool as effective as a good story.

Recognition and Rewards

I'm not going to address the specific issue of monetary compensation in this book because much has been written about this subject. If you want to attract and retain great people, you need to have a compensation structure and plan that allows you to do just that, with as many bells and whistles as necessary and appropriate to accomplish your goals. For the purpose of this section, I will assume you have done that. However, while that is necessary, it's not enough.

To really engage your employees, you need to constantly look for ways to recognize and reward them. Many companies have formal recognition programs, such as annual sales meetings where the best salesmen (e.g., the ones who break records) are brought up to the stage and given a trophy in front of all their peers.

I find that informal approaches to recognition are very powerful. Simply thanking a person for doing a great job goes a long way. So does remembering her name, or asking after a family member (a son who broke his leg, a husband who had an operation). Taking a small team out to dinner to celebrate the completion of a tough project has both short-term and long-term value. All these activities humanize you, make you more approachable, and enable people to be more willing to come and speak with you. And here's the bottom line: People like working at places where leaders are friendly.

*   *   *

Everything in this chapter boils down to one thing, as simplistic as it sounds: treat people as you would like to be treated. If you just did that, it would go a long way. This may sound easy, but it's hard for some people in high-level positions to treat people below them as equals. What executives need to understand is that it's not just about being a good person; it's also about good business. This is not a prescriptive, formulaic process—it's more of an altering of your mindset; it's learning to be interested in the people around you—finding out who these people really are, your fellow human beings. This is something that becomes grooved with experience—like a great golf or tennis swing—it's not going to be productive if it's a random occasional event. This takes a real and continual interaction. And, like anything else that requires practice, the more you do it, the easier it gets.

CHAPTER SIX

CONNECTING WHERE IT COUNTS: MAKING LOVE TO YOUR CUSTOMERS

"There is only one boss. The customer. And he can fire everybody in the company from the chairman on down, simply by spending his money somewhere else."

—Sam Walton

The idea that a business needs to treat its customers well, and really understand their likes and dislikes, tastes, and habits, is so obvious it seems hardly worth stating. But oddly enough, many big companies fail in this area.

Fundamentally, you're in business to utilize the assets you have to generate a positive return on the investment made by your shareholders. To accomplish this, you sell a product or service to your customers and hopefully earn a profit on each transaction. It's really that simple. So why do many companies take their customers for granted or even treat their customers as annoyances?

There may be a good explanation for this unintentional behavior. As businesses have grown dramatically—in numbers of customers, products, services offered, and geographic markets—data and reports have increasingly become the primary tools for calibrating results and making decisions. To augment performance data, almost all companies use various forms of customer research, surveys, focus groups, mystery shoppers, and other techniques. These findings are informative, but often consist of aggregated data and use sophisticated statistical techniques to infer or explain what is going on with customers. While not inaccurate, this information is sterile and missing the tactile, personal element of the business itself—the basic and critical relationship between the company and its customer.

When Macy's opened its first department store in Herald Square, all the executives had their offices on the top floor of the building and were constantly walking the sales floors. They knew firsthand what products were selling and what their customers were saying. As the chain grew to hundreds of stores, it became virtually impossible to maintain that intimacy. Yet, that is exactly what leaders have to do—get with their customers and see what is going on.

To report on what is actually happening on the front lines, a correspondent like Richard Engel of NBC has to physically go to that location. To know what it's like to be buying a product from your company, you have to put yourself in the shoes of a customer. Sadly, few leaders really get this concept. For example, how many executives call their company's customer service number and experience hitting several numerical prompts and listening to music for ten minutes before speaking to an agent? How many retailers spend a few hours in their stores to witness their customers' shopping experiences? How many hospital CEOs have actually admitted themselves to their own emergency rooms to experience the pandemonium from the patient's point of view?

In each of these examples, the experience would be eye-opening and would trigger a series of questions, projects, and other activities to address the findings from these visits.

Is It Customer Satisfaction, or Inertia in Disguise?

I believe there is a substantial inertia factor in many company-customer relationships; that is, customers tend to stay with the companies they are used to dealing with, out of force of habit. Staying doesn't necessarily mean that they like the experience associated with dealing with that company. It could just be that their experience is generally okay, and they're not sure there is something new or better that warrants making a change. But when something occurs that may be upsetting, unpleasant, or generally not up to their previous experience or expectations, customers start to become more receptive to alternatives. If a competitor provides them with a great offer, then they may try it. If they like the new experience, then they're most likely not coming back to their old company. And here is something really interesting—when that happens, no one in headquarters either knows or cares—it's lost in the numbers. For example, a few years ago I had a very bad experience with my American Express Platinum card, where I had been a member since 1974. Fed up, I stopped all spending on that card and began using my Visa card instead. No one from American Express ever realized or cared that I had left, after forty years, and more important, no one reached out to me to ask why. They could have won me back, but they didn't try.

With certain products and services, the switching cost is high, which often keeps customers from changing companies. Let's say you have a checking account with Chase where your paycheck is directly deposited and all your bills are electronically paid from this account. You're not very happy, they've made a few mistakes recently on your monthly statement, and you've just received an interesting offer from Wells Fargo to open a new account. While it seems intriguing, you've got hours of work in front of you to switch all your accounts and ultimately decide you'll stay with Chase—even though you aren't that thrilled with them. They probably are unaware of your unhappiness, and you'll likely stay until something really bad happens and you can't take it anymore. (At that point, you are more than willing to change, regardless of how many hours of work you need to do.)

In my neighborhood, we had a Food Emporium supermarket—a very dated, dilapidated, and totally unappealing store. But it was the only one in our neighborhood. Then Fairway, an up-and-coming chain, opened a few blocks away and began to change the competitive landscape by providing customers with a wider choice of products at lower prices. One year later, Whole Foods opened a huge store in the same neighborhood with even more options for the shopper; they were very focused on meeting the growing demand for organic food. Within six months of Whole Foods opening, Food Emporium was losing customers so quickly that they decided to close this store. Another firm called Morton Williams, who owns a small chain of boutique supermarkets in New York City—each designed to reflect the needs of the individual neighborhood—saw the possibility of a great location. Despite these two powerful new competitors, they assumed Food Emporium's lease, modernized the store layout and product assortment, and introduced the store under their new brand. The store competes very effectively—it's the most convenient of the three, and it is now a pleasurable experience to shop there. Interestingly, Food Emporium is owned by A&P, which in addition to being the first major supermarket chain in the United States has the distinction of filing for bankruptcy twice.[1] The point is that Food Emporium was clearly not listening to their customers. They relied on inertia, which worked fine until new competitors entered the market.

Sometimes when I listen to leaders talking about their customers, it almost sounds as if they "own" them, and they are confident they will stay forever. The truth is, no one owns customers and you have to earn their trust and respect every day. And that is why you have to be connected with them, communicate with them regularly, and really understand what they want from you and how they feel about you.

Patagonia is one company that really gets it right. Founded by Yvon Chouinard in 1973, Patagonia sells high-end outdoor clothing. There is intense competition in this industry with companies like The North Face, Marmot, Columbia, Descente, Mountain Hardwear, and numerous others. Patagonia has its own retail stores and also sells its products in other major sporting goods retailers and specialty stores. In the interest of full disclosure, I have been buying their merchandise for twenty years and am a very happy and loyal customer. Everything they do is customer-centric. Their products are extremely well designed and well manufactured, and they last forever. They perform exactly as advertised. And the company provides seamless service throughout their channels of customer interaction—in store, online, and through telephone customer support.

They recruit staff for their stores who are perfectly suited to sell this clothing. Healthy, outdoorsy men and women, they are the embodiment of the brand. Most are familiar with the technical nature of some of the garments, and all seem very happy working for Patagonia. I have shopped in numerous Patagonia stores throughout the United States over the years and have seen the same characteristics and qualities in the staff wherever I am. In short, they hire people who want to work there.

I had a Patagonia ski jacket that I really enjoyed until the zipper broke. Not knowing what to do, I went to one of their stores in Manhattan and showed them my jacket. The salesperson, Jane, said it would be quite difficult to fix and they would replace it (even though I had bought it two and a half years before). As they no longer made that specific model, Jane walked me over to the jacket section and showed me a similar jacket, found my size and color, and gave it to me to try on. It was perfect, but I noticed the price was about eighty dollars more than what I had paid for the original jacket. It is important to mention here that up to this point, Jane had not asked me for my name, a sales receipt (which I no longer had), or anything else.

Jane took me back to the sales counter, asked for my name and zip code, found me in their database, scanned the jacket, placed it in a shopping bag, and wished me a good day. When I mentioned to her that the new jacket cost more than my original jacket, she gave me a big smile and said, "It's your lucky day."

Patagonia clearly did not have to make this exchange with me, but it actually does make sense, because I will likely be buying clothes from them for the next twenty years. Customer service is a one-on-one business, and you need to get granular and find ways to connect with your customers individually.

Reach Out and Touch Them

Rick McVey, founder, chairman, and CEO of the electronic bond trading company MarketAxess Holdings, is reshaping the way corporate bonds are being traded in the capital markets. His company, now sixteen years old, is a fully electronic low-cost exchange; it replaces the traditional trading platforms where individual bond trades were placed by phone and then processed through the participating banks.

When I interviewed him, one of the first things I asked was, "Do you stay close with your customers?"

McVey's response was immediate: "That is primarily what our sales team does. We have around one hundred clients, who are the really big buyers of bonds. We've integrated all of our systems into theirs, to make it easier for them, but also to make sure we are vitally important to them. When we come up with a new product, or acquire a new technology, we can integrate it onto our platform so that the client gets the benefit seamlessly. Because we bond so closely with our customers, they tell us who else is calling on them, so that's another way we get a fix on the market—and specifically those new companies who are seeking to take market share from us."[2]

McVey went on to say that many of their new products can be directly attributable to understanding their customers' pain points and being aware of other opportunities their customers are exploring. That type of intelligence is priceless.

Of the Five Engagement Principles, one of the most important—if not the most important—for leaders to adopt is connecting to the people who buy or use your product or service. So how do you begin connecting with your customers? There are three ways to find out what your customers want, feel, and think: Though phone interaction, field trips or onsite visits, and by being your own customer (putting yourself in their shoes).

CALLS

The people on the phone with your customers represent your company more than many leaders seem to be aware of. A customer's experience on the phone—whether it is in the normal course of business, or whether you are surveying your customers to gauge their level of satisfaction—is critically important to your business. Compare it to the treatment diners receive from waiters in a restaurant: good service means more customers, but poor service means you may not be in business for long.

Here is an example of how not to do it. I am a subscriber of the Verizon FIOS service and received a letter that my high-speed Internet service was being upgraded to the top speed possible and the monthly cost for my bundled service was going down. All I had to do was just call the phone number specified in the letter, and I would be all set. Clearly, this is something I was happy to do; sadly, the letter was the only good part of this story. When I called, I was asked why I was calling (Answer: because you sent me the letter), what was my problem (Answer: I didn't think I had one), and why did I want to change my service (Answer: I didn't). At the end of twenty minutes on the phone, a service call was scheduled for Verizon technicians to come to my home to replace certain equipment. I was offered time slots that were pretty wide (9 a.m.–12 p.m.) but my technician showed up at 12:30 anyway, complaining about traffic (bad traffic is normal for Manhattan, and is not a good excuse). After looking around, he informed me that my specific configuration (whatever that means) is ineligible for the upgrade, and that he cannot do anything. When I explained the whole process I went through, he said unapologetically, "They don't know what they're doing in sales—they just make calls, try to sign people up and make their numbers, and then we have to deal with all of that on our end." (I still have the original high-speed service, by the way.)

In contrast, here is an example of getting it right. We recently took a trip to Southeast Asia visiting Hong Kong, Vietnam, Cambodia, and Malaysia, and the itinerary— especially regarding flights—had to be tightly coordinated. A few days before we left, I called Cathay Pacific's customer service (via Skype) to clarify a few points about baggage allowance, check in times, etc. As soon as the agent accessed my records, she noticed one of our connecting flights did not allow sufficient time for us, and that it should not have been booked this way. She then said, "I understand we made this mistake, and I will get this fixed—please hold on." To straighten this out, she needed to consult with several different level supervisors, but came back on the line within fifteen minutes and told me everything was sorted out. In this case I was more than happy to have been put on hold while the agent went to such lengths to help me. Obviously

I was very thankful and was even more impressed when we checked in at JFK and the agent there apologized again for this potential mishap. They had actually noted the entire episode in my file, and this agent felt the need to explain again. That is connecting with your customer.

VISITS/FIELD TRIPS

As I have made clear in many other chapters of this book, it is essential for you to get out of your office and go to visit the places where your customers and employees interact. This gets at the very core of engagement. So how, practically speaking, do you arrange these field trips? Who should you speak to, what do you actually do, and what do you hope to discover?

Let's start with what you should not do. The joke in the United Kingdom is that the queen wonders why every place she visits smells like fresh paint. That's because every place she visits is freshly painted several days before she arrives!

A service center leader that I was meeting with described what seemed to be a corporate version of the queen's visit scenario—it was an account of how the former head of his division conducted her visits to the service center. "These visits were scheduled six months in advance and were highly orchestrated," he told me. "She flew in on the corporate jet with her entourage and had a limo take her and her team to our center. We served them donuts and coffee, made a bunch of presentations to them—they asked a few questions, and then they left." I asked him, somewhat incredulously, "Didn't they actually go into the center itself, walk around, talk to people and get a good sense of the operation, meet with the folks, etc.?"

"No," he replied, "and that's why the team was so unprepared for your visit. Even though you sent explicit instructions as to what you wanted to accomplish while you were here, they simply could not imagine another type of visit from someone at HQ."

Clearly, you should not just go through the motions. You'd be better off doing nothing (or going bowling) than to go on a superficial visit. Unless you really let your hair down and get in there—ask, look, engage—you will never discover what is really going on. Don't think of your visit as a guided tour. Don't just go to the area or department that your host wants to show you. In fact, whatever it is they want to show you is probably the area you least want to see. The folks you are visiting are motivated to put the best face on whatever the situation is, but your mission is to look behind the curtain. The more a visit is planned and choreographed, the less realistic it is, and therefore the lower its value. And the more senior in the organization you are, the more likely it is that the people organizing the visit will want to plan a great agenda for you—of what they think you should see.

To some extent, it can be self-serving—they don't want you to see anything that isn't perfect. In some cases, they have not seen it themselves, so it would be highly embarrassing for you to see something about their operation that they are unaware of. I've seen this kind of situation countless times.

On one memorable trip in Jakarta, James, the Indonesia country head for our company, took me to meet a very important client that I wanted to get to know. This was someone James assured me he had met several times. As we were driving to the client's office, I found it strange that James did not seem to know the directions. When we were introduced to the client (by the client's assistant), he graciously said to me, "It's very nice to meet you," and to James he offered, "It's very nice to meet you as well!" Needless to say the car ride back to our office was not the best conversation James and I had ever had.

The other type of constructive field trip is visiting a location where employees interact with customers—such as a retail store. When you make these visits, you do not have to pretend you are not an executive—this is not Undercover Boss. But you might just dress down a bit, to put everyone at ease. You are just there to observe—maybe help a salesperson put the shirt in the bag. Your goal is to listen to your employees talking to the customers, to watch people waiting in line to go into the dressing room, and to make mental notes when customers are bitching about how you don't have the color or size they want. Notice how they touch the merchandise. Then you can talk to your employees and find out what they think about the various issues at that store—about what is working and more importantly, what needs to be changed.

BE A CUSTOMER

Do unto others is an old adage, but it is rarely thought of in the context of company leaders and customers. The person at the very top of the organization should know what it is like on the other side of the exchange. Not too long ago I had the pleasure of speaking with Eli Zabar at his new Eli's Essentials store and café on Madison Avenue. The Zabar name is well known in Manhattan, and Eli split with his two brothers to form his own business in 1973 on the

East Side, when he opened the EAT gourmet food shop and café on Madison Avenue. Today Eli Zabar runs a very large retail, restaurant, and commercial baking company.

"I do believe in good service—everything I do in business, and outside of business, is an attempt to satisfy myself," he said. "I have zero patience to wait on line. My wife and I went to the museum to see a new exhibit, and if they told me they were giving away Rembrandt's while we were waiting on line, I still wouldn't want to stay on line. I'm extremely impatient—and I don't want anyone else to wait on line either."[3]

I asked Zabar how this affects what happens in his stores.

"If I see four people waiting on line in one of my stores, and I see an employee who is doing something else, the something else is the wrong thing. The right thing is for them to drop what they are doing and serve the next customer on line. If they are on the telephone, they need to excuse themselves from that activity, because the more important activity, unless it is an emergency, is to take care of the customers on the line, and to the other person to hold on or call them back."

"And how do your employees respond to this direction?" I asked.

"We all get so involved in the activity of the moment—it almost seems rude to the employee to tell them to stop what they are doing to focus on the customer. But it doesn't matter, because the customer is the most important part of the business."[4] Eli Zabar clearly gets it.

If you are the CEO or an exec of a chain of shoe stores, it would naturally behoove you to wander into one or your stores on a regular basis and (anonymously) buy a pair of shoes, to see what the experience is like. It's like spending the night in your own guest room. How else can you ever really know what your guest's overnight stay is like? Being your own customer is part of employing the Fresh Eyes principle—in this case it's the customer's eyes you are borrowing.

When I was chatting with Tom Hale of Backroads, I asked him, "When you go on a trip with your wife and kids, are you going on them like someone else would go?"

"Absolutely," he replied. "I go like any other guest would go. I've been on hundreds of trips; I still go on several trips every year. I'm having a great time, doing whatever is happening. However, my eyes and ears are always open. Always talking to the leaders. (I don't get into the kitchen anymore like I did the first five years and ask them why dinner isn't ready. That turned out to be a losing proposition.) But I never come back from a trip without observations on how that trip could be better; but more important, I come back with observations about how we can, company-wide, systems-wide, do things differently. Virtually every piece of information you will see on a trip originated from an observation I had personally on a trip. For example, there's 'straight talk.' That is a bit of branded information that is in a travel planner, something that has higher visibility, and is actually about something about that trip that not everyone in the world will respond positively to. We want to highlight these 'blemishes,' because we don't want people on the trip that have an expectation that is entirely different."[5]

Of course, most leaders are likely to be customers of their own products and services. If you are the CEO of Verizon, I highly doubt you have a cell phone contract with

AT&T. But there are subtleties and nuances. Often, companies identify board directors, top executives, and other influential people to receive "white glove" service. Simply put, these individuals do not experience what we mere mortals do. They have special customer service numbers, answered immediately by a real person, who generally can solve their problem on the spot. They experience all the good things and none of the bad. Unfortunately for them, they are not seeing an accurate picture of the company. Many years ago, when I found out about this practice, I basically turned off the "white glove" service because I thought everyone should experience both the good and the bad, which would help us fix whatever problems we had. Sounded good in principle, until a director called me to say that his wife was being "harassed" by one of our collection agents. It seemed she had run up a very sizable bill and was not paying us, which only became evident when we turned off the white glove service. Gently, I explained the situation to him, and duly embarrassed, he assured me it would be taken care of. The key takeaway from this story is: No white glove service for executives and directors!

*   *   *

If you are not already doing this, or you are but you are doing it only sporadically, here are several recommendations that relate to the Connecting principle. First and foremost, make a real commitment to spend a specific amount of time meeting with customers, either in groups or individually. These encounters should be scheduled in advance and should be no fewer than six times per year, for maybe two hours each. That is twelve hours for the year, a long day for most leaders, and an amount of time that you can certainly find in your schedule. By the way, you can also make impromptu visits as well, such as when I visited the Sears store in Miami—you can always find an opportunity to spend time with your customers.

This is an interesting, rewarding, and fun process—you are meeting with people who buy your stuff, and presumably are more happy than unhappy about what you offer them. Be open, let your hair down, and engage with them to find out what they like, what they don't like, what they would change, what else they would like you to offer, what annoys them about what you do, etc. You'll be amazed at what you learn—and I promise you this: you will learn more than you could ever imagine. Be sure to take good notes—I often come away from these sessions with most of a legal pad filled with great comments, suggestions, and ideas.

That was actually the easy part; now the real work starts. You need to report back to your leadership team about what you learned at your sessions. You need to see by their reactions how much is "new news" to them, because that in and of itself is a great diagnostic about how involved your team is. But the most important part of this report out, is the "so what, now what" portion. Specifically, what are you and your leadership team going to do to address the issues raised, what work needs to be done to address and improve these findings? How are you individually and collectively going to deal with the feedback you've received? This is the crucial part because unless you engage in this exercise, the report is merely a series of interesting anecdotes from the field.

To ensure this process goes full circle, the Meeting Czar will ensure that future reviews are calendared, which forces everyone to address the findings. In future quarters, the financial results will begin to reflect your responsiveness to your customers with lower attrition, higher sales and customer satisfaction, and higher Net Promoter Scores (NPS). Finally, six months later, you should be hearing different issues from your customers, as there is always something else to focus on—but you should not be hearing the same comments you heard last time. Otherwise, as Ricky Ricardo famously said in the *I Love Lucy* series, "Lucy, you've got some s'plaining to do!"

I really like NPS because it gets to the core issue. It asks anywhere from one to ten questions, all based on a scale from 1–10 (highest). The most important question to me is "Would you recommend this company, product, service to a friend?" The response to this one question encapsulates the entire customer experience. If I'm not entirely happy, I'm not going to recommend the company.

CHAPTER SEVEN

DO ASK, DO TELL—AND DO SHARE: REAL AND ACCESSIBLE INFORMATION FOR ALL

"A lack of transparency results in
distrust and a deep sense of insecurity."

—Dalai Lama

On the main entrance to my high school was the inscription Knowledge Is Power. At the time I was a student there, I really didn't pay attention to it, nor did I really understand its significance. Now, I do.

When it comes to being an engaged leader, making sure the information flows well is of paramount importance. Everyone needs to know what is really going on. Leaders need to get complete, accurate reports and then broadcast them in a timely manner to everyone who can benefit from this information. Companies base important decisions and action on measurements, on what has been tracked, but all too often the measurements are inadequate and/or the right things are not being measured. It's essential to evaluate the relevant information carefully and fully and then—equally as important—to disseminate the results as widely and as quickly as possible.

The current state of technology forces all companies to generate more information. Everyone has more. It might not be accurate, it might not be on time, and it might not be going to the people who actually need it, but everyone definitely has more. So the question is, how do you figure out who really needs what, when—and what can they do with it? How can you make sure that people are engaging in the right way? How do you empower your people to have the right information now to help them do their jobs better, and provide a substantially higher level of service to your customers?

Information is available on demand almost everywhere in the world. It goes without saying that this has transformed—and is continuing to transform—the world of commerce.

Thirty years ago, a tea farmer in a small village in India would load a cart pulled by a donkey and take the trek into the village, perhaps some twenty miles away, to sell his tea leaves. The distributor would inspect the leaves, determine their grade, and look at a printed price list that had been mailed from London (where tea prices are set) to determine how much to pay the farmer. Fast-forward to today. The farmer takes pictures of his tea leaves on his mobile phone, texts them to a wholesaler in Mumbai (who is online with the London market) who then fixes a price, tells him which wholesaler to deliver the leaves to, and deposits the funds into a mobile payment account owned by the farmer (who does not have access to a traditional bank account because he lives in a total cash world). Today's tea farmer not only gets paid twice as much but also has the convenience of his mobile payment account—and he really doesn't need the donkey any longer. This is a great example of how technology enables people to interact with less friction—with greater efficiency and effectiveness, and better results. On one hand, this kind of technology, which is both empowering and expeditious, is an enormously positive development for businesses. A recent Ericsson Mobility Report that was analyzed by the World Economic Forum showed that in 2015, the number of mobile phone subscriptions in the world reached 7.4 billion[1]—one hundred million more than the entire population on our planet, and this trend is only expected to continue with additional growth predicted.

On the other hand, how valuable is the information if it is two days old, or the inventory system does not adequately track sales as they occur, or people are not properly trained in how to use the technology? It's unbelievable how often these super powerful new tools do not work well, or are not applied correctly. Whether it's a medical organization whose central computer system makes the coordination of patient health-care information much more unwieldy or an automated phone system that annoys customers so much they hang up, the digital world only shows a reflection of the engagement level of the organizations that are utilizing it. The irony is that because computers make things so much easier, people assume that automatically means the information is better and it is utilized more efficiently. But so often that is not the case.

For example, how many times have you as a customer experienced something similar to the following scenario? A friend of mine named Kathy called Apple customer service because her text-messaging feature kept freezing on her iPhone. The agent diagnosed the problem and told her she would have to reset her phone to eliminate this issue going forward. She said she would need to reset two other features on her phone, but everything else would be okay. (It later turned out the new ApplePay feature was one of the things that needed to be reset, although the agent did not tell her about this on the call.)

As soon as Kathy reset her phone, she received an email from Capital One (one of her listed credit cards) to say that her ApplePay had been disconnected and directing her to call a special 800 number. Great, she thought to herself, *these guys really have it together, the way they knew right away the service had been disconnected.*

Kathy called Capital One and spoke with a woman named Tina, who was "happy to help her through this problem and get it cleared up right away." After Kathy explained what happened with resetting her phone, Tina asked, "Why did you cancel your account?"

"I didn't cancel the account, it was inadvertently disconnected because I had to reset my phone," Kathy reiterated.

The conversation deteriorated from there. Tina eventually told her, "I've never heard of this before. Are you sure you didn't cancel your card?" She posed other similarly ridiculous questions, and then asked if she could place her on hold while she investigated further.

At this point Kathy requested to speak with a "level two" technical supervisor. Enter Shirley, who asked more questions, placed her on hold a few more times, and finally pronounced, "This sure is a mystery." At the end of the call, Shirley said she would write up a work ticket so that their technical experts could look into this further, and assured her that they would get back to her shortly.

"So, in a few hours?" Kathy asked.

"Oh no, more like seven to ten days," Shirley replied. By now Kathy had been on the phone with the company for more than thirty minutes and was ready to go postal. It ultimately took around four hours for her to sort out this problem herself, and she never heard back from Capital One. (And P.S. she now uses a different credit card for her ApplePay.)

The point of this story is that the information, and its various connections and interfaces, in this case with a credit card provider, happened at lightning speed—but, the organization was unaware and not prepared to address the customer's situation. This is just as bad as not having the right information.

Whenever I hear a story like this, I always wonder whether anyone in a decision-making capacity at the company in question has any idea of the collateral damage that these types of customer encounters create. Do they realize that customers—who after all, have purchasing choices—will not put up with this type of behavior? In my friend Kathy's case, she decided to use another credit card, and Capital One lost a great customer for no reason.

Obviously no one in the company purposely sets up a system for customers to be frustrated, so there must be a cause behind this kind of occurrence. There is some area of disengagement to blame, some breakdown in a system. Somewhere in that department, there are missing links in communication. Someone in Apple should have alerted the customer to what might happen, and Capital One should not have treated an unintended consequence as the customer's problem. My point is that good information flow really has nothing to do with technology, per se. It's about how people are utilizing it.

There are three main areas of corporate disengagement as it relates to information flow: (1) having an entrenched silo structure, (2) the tendency of many leaders to withhold or ration information, and (3) poor tracking methods and systems.

Not only do many of the communication tools and practices employed by companies serve to convolute rather than to clarify, but also many leaders seem to have lost sight of the basic tenet that the more people know, the better they can do their jobs. To be an engaged leader is to be a transparent one.

Counteracting Corporate Silos

Often, people in different departments within companies are simply in the habit of erring on the side of nontransparency, of talking only among themselves instead of sharing information with other departments who need it. In fact, the lack of communication between the functional units of the company has become so common that most people accept it as the norm.

Within a given organization, the working units are usually structured by region—typically for sales activities—and by function (marketing, finance, operations, legal, etc.), and each one has its own leader, budgets, and goals. These units are referred to as "silos"—just like the grain storage tanks on farms, each one independent from the other. There is often friction between these silos, because their individual objectives frequently take precedence over the overall company objectives. This is where many problems are born. Silos are the opposite of interconnectivity, and therefore often an impediment to engagement.

For example, let's take a typical company. The job of the sales force is to go out and bring in new business, to sign up new accounts, and generate revenue for the company. Other departments become involved to bring these new clients on board and provide ongoing service and support. These departments are busy running their respective silo operations and are often more preoccupied with those activities than with coordinating efficiently with sales, or any other department. Each department has its own operations to run, its own goals, and all the people in that department are mostly concerned with how their own department will be affected. Companies seem to be fiercely addicted to divisions, to partitions.

In my role as a consultant, I was once approached by the CEO of a company whose business managed payments for other companies. Let's call this company the XYZ Company. XYZ's client companies were quite diverse in size, each having slightly different requirements and levels of complexity. Over the past few years, XYZ had grown very rapidly. They had made acquisitions; they had done very well, as far as the financials go. They came to me with a problem they had identified: It was taking way too long— about three months—to "on-board" each new client. They were getting a lot of pushback from these new clients who wanted to know why it took so long. "If you are so good," they said, "why can't we start in two weeks?"

"We want you to come in and tell us how to speed the process up," the CEO said to me.

I asked him what he had done so far about this problem. He explained they had found one area of the process they could improve, so that they could shave off three or four days, but that's where their effort had ended. I told him it sounded to me like this was more systemic—that it was an issue that probably ran deeper than the area they had identified.

"Funny you should say that, because I just found out from one of our guys that after we sign them up, we don't even talk to them for three to four weeks," said the CEO.

"What do you mean you don't talk to them for three to four weeks?"

"Apparently, we are just silent," he admitted.

Thinking this was a really strange way to treat new clients, I suggested they needed a better on-boarding process. When the salesman closes the deal, he should explain to the new client, in broad strokes, what would happen next: "You'll hear from us within ten days about what the implementation plan and calendar will be, who your project leader and contact person is, what you will need to do, what we are going to do," etc.

"Good idea," the CEO said.

It seemed so obvious to me that a new customer would want to know immediately what they had "bought." When you buy something, you want to feel good about it fairly quickly. So why hadn't the CEO and his colleagues at XYZ thought of this themselves? It turned out that it was mostly because the company's various units were not in sync.

In general, the sales organization would make a pitch for new business, and when it was successful, they'd enter into a contract with the new client company. The operations team was responsible for on-boarding the client and ensuring everything went smoothly for the implementation. The legal team's job was to ensure that the contract properly reflected the obligations and liabilities, and the finance team had to analyze the deal to validate that the company would achieve the targeted returns for this service. Even though everyone knew that each of these tasks was going to be performed for this new client, all the units of XYZ tended to work independently of one another, which made no sense.

Unfortunately, each silo was tracking how many days it took for their department to complete its own portion of the work but no one was tracking the time between the departments—the handoff time—or the total time it was taking to complete the process. It was as if someone put a stack of mail on your desk and it sat there for five days before you opened it, and you only started counting your department's time from the moment you opened the mail until it left your department. We quickly figured out that more than two of the three months was interdepartmental waiting time and that the actual work time was approximately three weeks! Further analysis showed that the waiting time was not because people were lazy, but rather because Department A would pass the information over to Department B before it had fully completed its work. This was fundamentally a silo issue, since these departments were not really speaking to each other but rather passing folders of work back and forth, again and again.

After speaking with the CEO, it had become clear that the breakdown in this process lay at the intersection of the silos; it was due to the lack of transparency, including key information, among the separate functional areas. Silos are rigid. In addition, the problem of the departments not speaking to each other was compounded by the company not keeping the client informed.

What should be a terrific experience (i.e., a sale, a new client, a new relationship) had turned out to be quite the opposite. This kind of scenario plays out every day in companies; however, it doesn't always have to be this way. Silos can be busted—the walls inhibiting communication and collaboration broken down.

This silo phenomenon is not limited to companies; it affects all organizations, including those in the academic sector. When I spoke with John Wilton, who worked with the World Bank for twenty-four years and is now UC Berkeley's vice chancellor for Administration and Finance, he told me about how he has been changing the academic version of the siloed system.

"When Berkeley first approached me for the job," Wilton said, "I thought to myself, you must be kidding. Why would I do that? The place faces serious deep-seated structural issues, from what I've read. But the selection panel was very candid about the situation they were in and said, 'We want someone to come in and help analyze the problems and help fix them.' They had suffered a series of damaging budget cuts from the state and had a very opaque, to say the least, budget information system, but they were aware of the problems and open to changing things, eager to turn the place around.

"When I first moved to Berkeley I found many of the administrative functions were siloed, just like systems had been at the World Bank. There were not tremendous synergies across units. Both organizations have a matrix structure, almost by necessity. In the Bank you would have different subject matter experts—in subjects such as agriculture, trade policy, etc.—on one side. On the other side you have regional or country expertise—people who know about Asia or Indonesia, etc. At Berkeley, there are a number of matrix type structures: for example, those responsible for teaching and research on one side, and then those responsible for running the place—the administration—on the other side. And in many cases, there is no 'line of sight' into a business unit's overall budget. People focused on incremental changes of some historically determined subset of the revenues and expenses. It was a system that had grown over many years and made running the place very difficult. As a part of this system, many transactional-level administrative services were decentralized to the academic units, with each unit having developed their own way of doing things. This created a need for a lot of manual work to make different systems 'talk to one another,' which created errors and made the standardization of systems or training impossible."[2]

A report by Bain consultants had recognized the same problem and recommended establishing centralized services for transactional work. Wilton explained that implementing this recommendation was complex and politically difficult. People were used to having their own people down the hall and those people liked their homegrown systems, even though they were costly, produced errors that the center then had to fix, and did not allow for any standardization. As Wilton went on to explain, "Aside from these issues one difficult problem was how to finance the new Campus Shared Services center. Due to the crazy legacy university budget system, staff in the academic units was paid from various different sources depending on what fraction of their work was attributed to this or that activity. Moving the people and the budgets that funded them was going to be very costly and complex."

"So how did you make it work?" I asked him.

"I asked the budget office to compute how much each

academic school or college spent on the services we wanted to move," said Wilton. "The answer was remarkably similar, about 2 percent of their budget. Thus we decided to move the people, but not the budget and then impose a 2 percent tax on total expenditures, which would finance shared services. This approach greatly reduced the complexity—the budget office can do this once a year in a couple of hours—and the result at the aggregate academic organizational unit is the same. It's a good example of finding an innovative way around an entrenched system that you often can't really fix. You have to discard it and do it completely differently. You have to simplify things, get rid of the clutter, cut the Gordian knot. The same is true for the whole incremental budgeting system . . . it makes no sense."

Another example was the timekeeping system. "Believe it or not," Wilton said with a smile, "Berkeley had sixty-one timekeeping systems for payroll/leave accrual/sick leave purposes, etc. One method in an academic unit was for people to write their time on Post-it notes and stick them on the door of the timekeeper, who would, periodically, take the notes off the door and enter the information into their local system. Funnily enough, the audit of the different systems showed the Post-it note method to be one of the more accurate! I used to make the joke that it worked quite well—as long as it wasn't windy!" He eventually moved everyone to one automated computer-based system but told me it was an extremely difficult and time-consuming process. People liked what they were use to.

"With some change you have to be patient," Wilton said. "In some cases we were forced by circumstances to centralize people and legacy systems that were inadequate and costly. One has to realize that the act of centralizing doesn't solve the problem in itself, but having put them in one place you can begin the long and difficult process of rationalization, have the systems run by people that actually have the expertise, etc. You have the capacity to push through the reforms." Wilton adopted a pragmatic and time-consuming approach with multiple ways of obtaining feedback and iterating with different parts of campus. But by removing these activities from their silos it did enable Berkeley to begin the process of change that was long overdue.

My basic methodology for breaking down silos requires clarity of purpose, full transparency, some basic principles, and accountability.

For this to work effectively, it is essential to identify the right key performance indicators (KPIs) to track within and between departments or units. For example, an integrated goal might be to generate one thousand new sales next year, with 90 percent of new customers activated within three weeks, and the balance within five weeks. This goal will necessitate tracking key metrics and each affected department working together to achieve the integrated goal.

Many companies, realizing the negative outcomes silos create, are actively seeking ways to promote cross-functional working groups—and more directly, eliminating the silos specifically. For example, in December 2015 the *Wall Street Journal* reported that the Publicis Groupe has decided to overhaul its structure and shuffle its leadership group to drive better financial results after years of disappointing performance.

"We have decided to get rid of silos," said company Chief Executive Maurice Lévy. "I'm obsessed by this. Silos are counterproductive in serving our clients well."[3] In many ways, silos are the complete antithesis of the Five Principles of Engagement.

HERE ARE SOME GUIDELINES I'VE FOUND USEFUL:

- DECLARE THE END OF SILOS: Perhaps the most important action you can take as the leader is to declare that you are running an integrated company and that each department's goals and operations are only there to support and grow the entire business. You need to explicitly state that silo-like behavior is not acceptable and that leaders who behave that way will not progress within the company. In other words, you need to make it clear that you are looking for team players and not leaders of fiefs. This mandate needs to be reinforced in every interaction—including meetings, one-on-one discussions, email, etc. Your messaging and actions will set the tone for creating an open, collaborative, nonsiloed organization. And you need to be vigilant in "calling out" individuals who are not adopting the right behavior on issues big and small.

- UTILIZE CROSS-FUNCTIONAL TEAMS: It is vital that everyone who might be affected by a project or new policy be involved in every stage of that project. Often, someone will decide it is enough to send out a simple email (assuming that everyone is going to be able to figure out from the email what their roles and responsibilities are) when having a cross-functional meeting is what's needed. The Meeting Czar (see chapter 2) will ensure that all participants needed for a discussion are present and that all the materials presented in advance of the discussion reflect the needs and concerns of all the departments involved. Cross-functional teams serve to reinforce the interconnectivity of all departments and can cut many potential silo issues off at the pass.

- DISCOURAGE BLIND CARBON COPYING (BCC): The very nature of bcc suggests that the sender is not willing to share the information with everyone involved—itself a topic of concern. One simple way I deal with this behavior is to "suggest" the elimination of bcc in all email. When I receive a bcc copy of an email, I send my response to all recipients with a suggestion that they work this issue out together. Duly embarrassed by this, senders of these email messages usually realize it is better to just cc all the appropriate people and eliminate any potentially hidden agendas.

- SET INTEGRATED GOALS: The goal-setting process needs to be one that guarantees the right balance between departmental goals and company-level goals. I have seen many, many variations of this basic principle, and of course there is no generalizable correct formula. At the highest levels within an organization, the vast majority of the leader's focus should be on overall company goals; that company-as-a-whole percentage shrinks as you move downward within the organization. A leader at a lower level in the company has a high degree of control over her department, but very little ability to affect the company as a whole.

Unclogging the Pipes: How to Stop the Rationing of Information

Many leaders have a tendency to withhold information rather than share it—for a variety of reasons, both conscious and subconscious. This stingy mode of interacting translates into a lack of transparency and creates mutual mistrust and unnecessary stress.

Throughout history, it's been a part of human nature to try to control other people by withholding or limiting access to information. The best example of this is North Korea, which has two government-controlled TV stations and virtually no Internet access available to its citizens. For all intents and purposes, they are living on a different planet. This isolationist behavior allows Kim Jong Un in Pyongyang to effectively control everything his people see, know, and experience. They only see what he wants them to see. That is the ultimate control of information, and in this case, allows a repressive regime to exist. This will only last until an open Internet arrives in North Korea, at which point the citizens will realize they have been living in a different world—and they will want what everyone else has.

On a much smaller scale, in the business world, managers often exert their real and perceived "power" by controlling the flow of information. If I know something that you don't, then you need to ask me for that information, which at some level subordinates you to me. It could be something very confidential ("Are we signing a contract with Adidas or Nike?") or it can be very simple ("When is the new line of running shoes going to be available in our store?"). Or the information may not even be that important. It could just be that I want to know more than you.

This instinct to withhold exists not only in the business world. It's a part of the human condition. In other words, just because you are a vice president does not mean that you aren't subject to all the psychological tugs and pulls that all people are subjected to. Take this mundane example.

John and Jane are going to dinner. John has chosen a restaurant in the West Village in Manhattan. (They are on foot.)

"So where is this place?" asks Jane, who is not wearing the most comfortable shoes.

"Not far," John answers.

"No really, how many blocks is it?"

"Not too many."

"Why won't you just tell me how far away it is?" says Jane, starting to feel annoyed.

"Don't worry," says John.

"I'm not worried!!" Jane says, feeling increasingly frustrated. "But why won't you tell me?"

"We're almost there," John says, quickening his pace.

"STOP!!" demands Jane. "Where is the damn restaurant?!"

Sheepishly, John finally admits that he is not really sure where it is.

"Jesus." Jane shakes her head, whips out her phone, and pulls up Google maps. "Why didn't you just say so?"

What this story illustrates is that sometimes information stinginess is not overtly about power but rather is about fear or insecurity. Perhaps people are afraid for someone else to know how much they don't know about an issue, or maybe they are nervous they have not completed something on schedule. Maybe a leader is simply trying to get through a project quickly and thinks explaining too much to others will slow him down. Perhaps he thinks if he shares uncomfortable or negative information, it might depress or stress out subordinates and cause them to have serious concerns about their job or the company—or that they will become preoccupied with those issues instead of doing their job. There can be many reasons why a person chooses to withhold information. But no matter what the reason, it gives the withholder some sense of control. People who use information as a method of control feel more secure—for a while, at least, until something bad happens as a result of their information hoarding.

Being nonforthcoming in business may stem from the more traditional command-and-control leadership style honed by the military and widely adapted to business in the twentieth century. In this model, leaders were typically not questioned, but rather blindly obeyed. It is also deep in our human DNA not to want to let others in on everything we know (or don't know.) So we have to retrain ourselves to be open, knowing that openness breeds success.

While some managers and leaders act like Kim Jong Un and others are totally transparent, the majority operate somewhere in the middle. The fact is that, in general, the more information flows, the better. Let's say you need to lead a group over a hill. If you tell everyone the truth about why you need to get over the hill and exactly why you need their help to do it, most people will pull up their socks, tighten their shoes, and go for it. But if you don't let them in on the full situation, they will be less likely to figure out what is needed to accomplish the mission, and probably none of you will make it over the hill.

One common area where nontransparency hurts business is in sales. Traditionally, the information flow of sales pipelines that get converted into sold accounts has always been a bit of a black box. In some cases, salespeople did not want to share the names of these prospects, for fear their colleagues might take the leads instead of them. (If you've ever seen David Mamet's *Glengarry Glen Ross*, this is the premise of the whole play/movie.) Sometimes, the salesperson—for one reason or another—was not even calling on the account but was still forecasting that the business would come in. (Even though you obviously cannot close a deal if you do not actually speak with the prospect.) These and many other behaviors made it difficult for senior leaders to clearly project sales and revenue.

SalesForce.com, founded in 1999, is one organization that enables and encourages open sharing/transparency policies. It describes itself as a cloud-based applications company and has a market capitalization of just under

$50 billion.[4] One of its first and biggest applications allows sales forces to track results of both existing customers and prospective customers, while enabling everyone in the organization to "see" into the data—in other words, full transparency.

When properly implemented and managed, Salesforce provides real-time information from top to bottom in an organization. For example, perhaps a CEO is meeting with a major customer. Using Salesforce, he is able to see the extent of the current relationship with the client, the nature of new business proposals that his organization is currently pitching, a list of all the key players on the client team, and any other relevant information. Imagine the nature and power of the conversation of that upcoming meeting, when it has been informed by the depth and breadth of this kind of information.

Business leaders can also use Salesforce to manage their sales organizations—to break down barriers, clarify communications, enable other parts of the company to assist in pitches, and generally improve overall performance. The use of this type of information requires everyone to be engaged, because everyone else in the organization is seeing the same information—which is thorough and current. It is impossible to opt out and hide; this speaks to the heart of transparency. A system like this counteracts people's natural instinct to hoard information and instills in them an understanding of the connection between the sharing of information and successful results.

I worked with one company that is now really getting it right. This company had a fairly common problem. They had lots of information, from hundreds of reports, and yet no one quite knew what was going on—not even to answer basic questions. The reporting systems were based on various production and service activities, and there was no interconnectivity of results. The reports all cut off at different times of the day (midnight, 9 p.m., 2 a.m.), so the answer to "How many did we sell yesterday?" varied, depending on which report you looked at.

The CFO decided to sort this out, and hired a financial "temp" to collect all reports, analyze them, learn who received them, what they did with them, etc. After a few months, it was clear that most people receiving the reports didn't look at them. Other people transferred the data to excel spreadsheets and created their own reports, which then got sent to other departments. The proliferation of these homemade reports spread like weeds, and of course, these reports were used as source information for yet another batch of reports.

There was no "single source of truth" and so people spent their time either debating the accuracy of the numbers or identifying the need for another report. Of course, the one thing no one was doing was taking action. The team decided to build a "data warehouse"—a single repository of data that houses all the source information of the company, regardless of where it originates from, onto a single platform. Once all the information is mapped to all other related information in the company, a series of application tools enables the creation of standard reports, customized reports, and the ability to have the information delivered to an iPhone, iPad, or a laptop. It's accurate, timely, and single-sourced. Everyone throughout the company is looking at the same information, even though departments might see their information in a specifically structured, or custom, format.

Now the conversations are about what the information means, and what they can do to act on it, rather than debating the accuracy of the information. Everyone is happy, except for the people who liked the old reports—because that entire process was shut down.

What Does Targeted Tracking Look Like?

Once you've addressed the silo problem and stopped the rationing of information, its time to focus on targeted tracking.

Tracking is one of those areas where a lack of engagement can really have a negative effect. Quite often companies either don't measure things, or—even more often—they measure the *wrong* things. Companies tend to track the things that are quantitative in nature rather than qualitative.

Also, most people end up doing only what their superiors review with them. Let's say the boss says to you, "How many customer service agents did you talk to this week? You were supposed to talk to eight." And you say, "Yes, I talked to eight." The boss might say, "Okay, do more next week." Then next week you report that you talked to ten. The boss says "good." The problem is that no one is keeping track of *what* these ten customer service agents reported to you. Whether the boss is asking "How many pairs of shoes did you sell today?," or "What's the ninety-day order backlog for our newest jet engine?" subordinates really have no choice but to respond in the way they've been instructed to. Unfortunately, it's usually an extremely reactive way of measuring things. We need to change the process—to ask more open-ended questions rather than those that simply have numeric answers; we need to inspire a more authentic, more engaged kind of tracking.

A company can change the way tracking and sharing information is done. As always, it starts with engagement.

* * *

There is a boutique food store a few blocks from my apartment where management has amazing interactions with their employees. Every morning, just before 7 a.m. when they open the doors, the manager stands in the middle of a circle with all of her staff around her—every employee. I see this every time I'm on my way back from the gym, and a few times, I just stood outside watching, even though I wasn't aware of what was being said. Sometimes they wave at me, probably wondering, *Who is this crazy guy watching us?* One day I waited for them to open and went to see the manager to find out what she was doing. I said, "I see you every day having these meetings before you open, what's that all about?"

Marie, the manager, said, "Look, we have about twenty-five people working here, and we're open fourteen hours a day. There is always something going on, good, bad, or otherwise. I need them to know everything I know—what's new, what's missing, what specials are we offering, and so on. I then ask them what they think, or about anything that happened yesterday that we need to know. It's just a quick session so that everyone is on the same page. It takes under ten minutes, and I could not imagine running this place without it."

This is a great example of being open, letting everyone know what they need to know in order to be successful—that

HERE ARE MY SPECIFIC RECOMMENDATIONS:

- Begin with an outside-in view. Ask yourself, "What are the key performance indicators (KPIs) that drive the performance of this business?" Generally speaking, this will be somewhere between ten and fifteen items. These measure financial performance (sales, margins, inventory, cash, earnings), risk and compliance, and customer satisfaction. KPIs begin at the corporate level and of course need to be built from the ground level up. Properly reviewed and discussed, these KPIs provide tremendous visibility to everyone in the organization about what's working, what's not working, and where potential opportunities and issues are; and will show early warning indicators for risk. Choosing the right KPIs necessitates cross-functional cooperation, and having a single source of information eliminates many of the problems discussed earlier in this chapter.

- Try to choose KPIs that reflect the core elements of the Five Principles: fresh eyes, connecting, hot buttons, speed, and transparency. While it is important to capture financial results, it is equally important to track indicators that relate to your employees and customers.

- Perform a complete review of existing reports, with the goal of identifying those that really do not add value and eliminating them. Managers look at these reports out of habit, but in many cases the reports are not providing them with any meaningful information. It is often like looking at the weather report from last week—who cares if it was sunny then when it's pouring today?

- Consider investing the time and money to build a data warehouse (DW). To put it simply, DW is a capability that allows an organization to map and link all of its various independent systems into one central location. This enables a single source of data to deliver information and reports throughout the organization, either on a routine basis or on demand. The cost and time to implement this capability will be more than offset by the enormous performance improvement.

day. Who's out sick and who has to cover? Why is it the croissants will arrive thirty minutes late? Describing the amazing soup the chef has prepared for the day. No secrets, and everything on the table to allow everyone to do their jobs well, informed with the latest, best information available. How empowering is that?

The best companies today, whether they are large or small, share as much information as they can among their leaders and employees. They know that knowledge is power and that, when they are properly trained, employees will exceed their expectations in responding to customers' needs.

CHAPTER EIGHT

ADOPTING THE
MO OF START-UPS

"Only the paranoid survive."

—Andrew Grove, former CEO, Intel

Start-ups have a great advantage. Once they make the decision to start their business, they operate at full throttle almost immediately. Of course there are dozens of concerns—hiring key employees, raising initial funding, building the technology, and finding initial customers, to name a few—but once they start, the word "no" never seems to come up. They know that if they do not build their business, and quickly, they'll have nothing—so it becomes a fight for their life from day one. Like speedboats, they are built only to go fast.

Established companies are very different, especially when they are large, successful, and have been in business for decades or longer. If start-ups are like speedboats, these older companies are more like modern day cruise ships—with ten decks, three swimming pools, a rock climbing wall, and a five thousand-passenger capacity. The older successful companies have great attributes, but they often fall victim to their own successes. Inertia plays a big role. And like cruise ships, their size makes it harder for them to accelerate and even harder to stop.

There are several common characteristics present in many established companies that seem to evolve over time—even though no one in these companies has set forth an explicit strategy or plan to create them:

- Fundamentally, they don't know what their customers think of them. Remember: Just because customers continue to buy from you does not mean they are happy campers. Customers may not have discovered a good alternative yet or may not be annoyed enough yet. But the minute one or more of these conditions take hold, they're moving on. And when they do, does the company even know that they've left? Usually the answer is no.

- They take it on faith, often wrongly, that sales will continue to grow at the rate it has in the past, or at an even greater rate. This leads to making safer investments, which often means investing in new facilities for the same products and services, expecting continued growth (growth that often does not materialize) rather than investing in new initiatives.

- They have a tendency to dismiss new competitors as too small to make a significant impact on their large company—sort of like not bothering to swat at mosquitos. Why haven't Visa, MasterCard, and American Express launched new payment products like the ones created by PayPal, Square, Stripe, ApplePay, and countless others? Their customers are using these new products and starting to question whether and why they still are using a card when they can more easily pay with their smartphone. (Sometimes the more savvy older companies, after they see the start-ups gaining traction, create joint ventures with these firms or acquire them.)

- They have a historical bias toward owning assets rather than focusing on core competitive advantages. The upheaval created by the "sharing economy" is having profound impacts on more traditional companies. Airbnb has a market capitalization greater than Marriott,[1] and Uber is more highly valued than each of the three top domestic airlines (Delta, United, and American).[2] Yet in almost every city around the world, the taxi commissions, who license this form of transportation, are arguing fundamental protectionism for their members. They are not interested in the taxi customers but rather the taxi drivers—and this is exactly where companies like Uber are attacking. I was in Paris last year and took a taxi from the airport into the city. When I asked the taxi driver what he thought of Uber, he said, "I hate Uber." After he told me all the reasons why Uber was unfair, I asked him "Could you become an Uber driver, and if yes, would you earn more?" to which he quickly responded, "Of course I could be an Uber driver, and I would make more money." So I asked him the obvious next question, "So why don't you become an Uber driver," and he replied, "Because I hate Uber."

If you think back to my Five Principles of Engagement, start-ups are engaged almost by definition. Everything is new: fresh eyes is the whole raison d'être for starting the company; connecting is a given, because having fewer people in the organization working crazy hours means they are constantly communicating with each other; speed is a natural byproduct of their desire to get the business up and running; transparency is inherent in the fact that in a start-up there is no room to hide because they are all sharing a communal workspace; and hot buttons are the two to three essential levers needed to start the company. There is no way to not be engaged and actually start the business. But start-ups have their own issues, and most start-ups fail, mostly because they run out of money too early. Very often, entrepreneurs who fail go on to launch numerous other companies, learning from their experiences and believing that the next one will be the winner.

Having worked and operated in both traditional and start-up environments I can tell you the differences are like night and day. Like most things in life, the right answer is a balance—harnessing the best of both worlds. But the three most important start-up characteristics that every company needs to embrace are a will to win, the ability to pivot, and speed.

There Is No "No"

If you start with the belief that you will win, the corollary of that is that there can be no "no." What this means is that every conversation in the organization is about problem solving. It means hiring the right people who not only have the requisite skills but who will also fit within the emerging

HERE ARE SOME FIXES TO TAKE THE "NO" OUT OF YOUR TEAM:

- At a scheduled meeting, ask your leadership team to come prepared to talk about the three biggest competitive concerns they have—and how they plan to counter them. This will immediately show you how deeply rooted and comfortable, or uncomfortable, they are. You need to move them out of their comfort zone to where the team engages in a meaningful discussion about real concerns. Only then can you begin to have a discussion about how you can take the offense and develop plans to combat these potential incursions. Keep the discussion centered on solutions, not problems.

- At another meeting, ask each member to define weak points in their colleague's businesses or operations, and what they would to do fix them. (This is similar to the switching jobs method in chapter 5, but without the actual switching.) Because everyone is going to be engaged in this process, it's fair play. I've seen leaders who have been previously very polite and reserved with each other suddenly reveal their concerns in a very honest and straightforward manner, often with very good suggestions for improvement. In order to make this work, you need to tell it like it is; you need to put the cards face up on the table. Remember, this is not summer camp.

- In your next meeting, or one-on-one discussion with your leaders, refuse to accept a no answer from anyone—no matter what the question is. Take the answer "no" completely off the table. Force them to find a way to deal with the issue in a positive manner. This may be difficult, as they may be out of shape in the area of positivity—but like working out regularly, it gets easier the more you do it.

culture. It means the roadblocks that inevitably appear are treated like challenges to be overcome. It means that if customers react poorly to the product, the product needs to be reconfigured or replaced rather than saying the customer doesn't get it. It means that any and all deadlines are met, because the consequences of missing a deadline could be fatal. All of this is because most start-ups started with nothing, and in a sense, have little to lose.

Compare that point of view with conversations I've heard over and over in large companies: "We missed our budget by 4 percent this quarter, but we'll probably make it up next quarter," "We did a little research on that new company you told us about, and they only have ten thousand customers—not a big deal," "Our customers are going to love the new dispenser on our product, and sales will go up at least 8 percent to 10 percent next year." These companies have a base business to protect and tend to be more introverted in their outlook (inside out) rather than start-ups that look at the needs of the marketplace first and foremost (outside in).

The Pivot

One of the great characteristics of start-ups is that they learn to pivot. What this means, simply, is that if the business you launched is not working as desired, you change it. Generally the changes are not small and require taking many deep breaths before you execute them. You are not sure the changes are going to work, but you are fairly confident that staying as you are will result in failure. And like most things, speed plays a critical role with pivoting.

Netflix, led by founder and CEO Reed Hastings, is a great example of a company that continually questions its business model and communicates with its customers all the time. The short story is that the company was founded because Reed was tired of paying late fees for his VCR rentals and decided to offer a service to mail DVDs for a flat fee to his customers, who could send them back whenever they wanted to. By 2000, the company had three hundred thousand subscribers and offered to sell the company to Blockbuster, who by then had over 7,700 stores. Blockbuster declined to buy the business.[3] In 2007, Netflix took the process one step further and began delivering video on demand (VOD) service, despite the fear of cannibalizing its own DVD-by-mail platform. This new service allowed the company to begin to monitor and understand the behavior of its customers online while simultaneously lowering its distribution costs. In September 2011, it rebranded its DVD service as an independent subsidiary called Qwikster, and one month later announced Qwikster was dead based on an overwhelming negative reaction from its customers. In 2013, the company reached thirty-two million subscribers (three million more than HBO)[4] and launched its original content series *House of Cards*. Here are a few key metrics about Netflix as of December 2015:

- $48 billion market capitalization[5]
- 69 million global subscribers[6]
- Highest level of customer satisfaction over competitors, receiving a 4.1 rating (on a 1–5 scale) compared with Amazon Prime Video and HBO Go (both at 3.4)[7]

And Blockbuster? Following a raft of different owners (including Viacom) acquisitions (Gamestation), and financings, the company was delisted from the New York Stock Exchange in July 2010 and filed a Chapter 11 bankruptcy petition in Sept 2010. In 2011, Dish Network bought the company's remaining assets for $320 million and decided to close the remaining stores in 2013.[8] ABC News reported that the very last DVD to be rented at a Blockbuster store was, ironically, a film called This Is the End.[9]

Large companies are much less likely to do what Netflix did. Rather, they are more comfortable just tweaking things—add a little here, take off a little there, saying to themselves, "We are doing something, right?" It is clearly visible years later that many products have been repeatedly tweaked. But tweaking is definitely not pivoting, and the relatively minor changes usually don't register that much with the customer. Eventually the company runs out of ideas for new ways to tweak the products.

In comparison to pivoting, let's look at an example of continued tweaking. A Canadian company named Research In Motion launched the BlackBerry in January 1999. In 2002, it introduced the 5810, which featured a revolutionary device that included a QWERTY keyboard for typing email, a phone, a calendar that would sync up with your Outlook system, and a system to "push" email to subscribers so that for the first time, you were able to be continually connected to your office. Popular with businesspeople, and specifically "road warriors" the company grew dramatically, and its 2007 annual report stated that it had eight million subscribers.[10] BlackBerry, or "crackberry" as it was also called, became a corporate status symbol, and the company behaved as if the market was exclusively theirs.

Enter Apple, who launched its iPhone in July 2007, offering a beautifully designed product utilizing a new iOS platform that would allow a customer to make calls, text, email, listen to music on iTunes, take photos, look at photos on iPhoto, and more. A *CNET* article by Tom Krazit said, "That's amazing progress in a year from a company that had never participated in this market before. Phones and computers are finally coming together, after years of promises of convergence. And Apple will definitely play a leading role in the definition of that market over the next several years, having earned the right during the first year of the iPhone."[11] In 2008, Apple created its App store, where developers could create all kinds of games, productivity tools, and a host of other exciting features.

Similar activities were happening at Google, which acquired a company called Android in 2005. In November 2007, Google announced the formation of the Open Handset Alliance that included device manufacturers, wireless carriers, and chipset makers. The first Android device was released to the market in October 2008,[12] slightly more than one year after the iPhone introduction.

The rest, as they say is history. BlackBerry continued to grow, launch new features, handsets, and even began offering some apps. Apple, Samsung, LG, and others expanded the consumer market at breathtaking growth rates while simultaneously beginning to convince corporate users (like me) that there was something better, and more fun, than the BlackBerry.

Fast-forward to 2013; the market had changed dramatically.

Both Apple iOS and Android each had about 800,000 apps available to their customers,[13] while BlackBerry had

135,000.[14] Developers of apps, in prioritizing their work, chose to design products that would work on the two major platforms (Apple iOS and Android) so that they could sell more apps.

BlackBerry, in September 2013 announced a layoff of 40 percent of its workforce, reduced the number of models sold, and sold the company to Fairfax Financial.[15] According to the research firm IDC, BlackBerry, which had a reported US market share of 45 percent in 2009, saw its market share fall to 2.1 percent. The most recent IDC report in 2015 on worldwide smartphone market share shows Android at 82 percent, Apple iOS at 14 percent, and BlackBerry at .3 percent.[16]

The moral of this story is that a series of tweaks in the face of relentless competition does not work. What's required is a full, courageous pivot.

Carpe Diem: The Importance of Speed

I've never met a leader who says to his team, "Let's move slowly." In fact, most companies think they are moving quickly—it's just they are not. Corporate time is typically measured in months, quarters, and years, whereas start-ups think in hours, days, and weeks. It drives me crazy when I see leaders who believe they have time to ponder. When I find myself in situations where leaders are not moving, I often say to them, "If your house is on fire, now is not the time to decide where to build the new fire station." In many cases, as I have discussed earlier in this book, organizations are viewing things from the inside out. Looking from the outside in is the right mindset, one that forces you to think and move quickly.

As Mario Andretti, the famous racecar driver, once said, "If things seem under control, you're just not going fast enough"—and this is a man who knows what fast means. As recently as ten years ago, it took a lot longer to design and launch products, or even companies for that matter. But with improvements in technology, unlimited resources, and cash available globally, things can happen much more quickly. There are hundreds of companies that have been written about—like Sony, Kodak, Radio Shack, SkyMall, and others—who did not realize that the pace at which they were moving, while it might have sufficed earlier, was no longer going to work in today's world. They sat by and watched their vaunted products, and in some cases the companies themselves, wither on the vine. In the past, corporate demises took decades, but today the same thing can happen in months and years.

I really don't think leaders intentionally want to move slowly; but there are several factors preventing them from moving fast. Fear is clearly an element that often leads to endless requests for analysis, meetings, studies, and other measures, whose sole purpose is to minimize risk. While some of that may have value, the problem often is that the analysis is too internally focused, and the time spent reviewing the information exacerbates the fundamental problem itself. I often say that perfection never happens and that "85 percent of very good, now" is a much better plan of action than 100 percent of perfect, which may never happen.

Another common impediment to speed is being wedded to a plan and to the planning process in general. These annual plans, typically formalized in the fall of the prior year, take on a life of their own and often are the primary element in determining executive compensation. Leaders tend to want to stick with the plan even in the face of new developments. Often I will hear a leader, in response to a new development say, "Let's bake that into next year's plan." This assumes you will be able to weather the storm until then.

When I was talking with Tom Hale, he emphasized the importance of the Speed engagement principle. "Speed is very, very important at Backroads," he said. "We had a survey we still do at the end of our busy season (right around the end of October), which goes out to all employees—office staff and leaders, etc.—and we get a lot of feedback on that. I find that to be an extreme bottleneck to moving forward quickly. I also find certain management team–type retreats to be a bottleneck, because we tend to collect topics to address them. And so just more recently we are trying to deconstruct both of those bottlenecks to move more quickly. A lot of that does emanate from me, because I can never do something fast enough. There is a certain part of me that expects that of others; I get a lot of ribbing and jokes about how I will say some ridiculous thing about how fast something can be done. But sometimes it can be done pretty darn fast when it has to be done. So we try to move towards that."[17]

It is probably unreasonable to expect a large organization to operate like a start-up for all the reasons mentioned. Yet it is possible for big companies to adopt some key elements of what makes start-ups so unique. First and foremost, leaders need to decide that they will embrace a few start-up attributes and start modeling those behaviors at every opportunity.

At weekly meetings, leaders need to listen differently to what is being said with a keen ear to pick up on it when people quote longer time frames than are needed, plans for extensive analysis (i.e., paralysis), and other common slowing-down elements. Instead, leaders need to ask: "What needs to be accomplished in order to make this decision within two weeks (or one week, or three weeks)?" Then they need to have a discussion as to why the recommendation says it is going to take four months. In other words, it's important to instill a sense of urgency, so that people do not err too much on the side of being slow and careful. People need to remember they are in a war, not at a tea party.

Another tool to apply is the "so what, now what" question. Too often, someone will describe a situation, as if he was only an observer, and then move on to another topic. You need to stop the discussion, say, "Hold on a second; let's go back to the other subject. I need you to tell me specifically how and when you plan to successfully address this issue." Right there.

Though he is no longer a start-up CEO, Eli Zabar is someone whose way of doing business has a lot in common with a start-up mentality. Everyone in the company knows every aspect of the business; everyone wears all the hats. And speed is essential.

"My impatience does lead to speed," Zabar said, "though I know I'm probably not going to get it right initially. The first time typically turns out to be a test run. We learn from the experience and fix whatever needs fixing in the second phase, then do it again in the third phase, if necessary. Perfect doesn't exist," he went on with a broad smile. "We are totally self-contained and do everything ourselves.

We have our own trucks, drivers, mechanics, refrigeration people—everything—because we want to make sure it's done right, and we want it done fast. We found that this is the only way we can operate."[18]

Of course, another way to adopt the principle of speed is for companies to collaborate. As reported in *Crain's* in December 2015, JPMorgan Chase, the biggest bank in the United States, is partnering with OnDeck Capital in order to dramatically speed up the process of providing small dollar loans (loans typically less than $250,000) to their small business clients.[19] By combining Chase's relationships and lending experience with OnDeck's technology platform, they can offer almost real-time approvals and same- or next-day funding. Chase will provide OnDeck's technology platform to its four million small business customers—meaning loans that currently take days or weeks to fund will now be made within minutes or days. Clearly this collaboration better serves the needs of the small business borrower. It is a perfect marriage between the customer strength of JPMorgan Chase and the technology platform of OnDeck Capital. It's a case of a traditional company keeping up with the times rather than going the way of RadioShack.

Increasingly, large companies that understand and appreciate the need for acting like start-ups are proceeding along three simultaneous tracks: finding ways to get their own organizations to ban the word "no," learning how to successfully change course in a storm, and training themselves to keep their foot firmly on the gas pedal.

CHAPTER NINE

WHY PLAYING NOT TO LOSE IS NOT THE SAME AS WINNING

"A ship in harbor is safe; but that is not what ships are built for."

—John Augustus Shedd

Initiative's Invisible Enemy

As I was driving into Manhattan for work one Friday morning in January of 1987, I was startled to hear Mayor Ed Koch say on the radio, "If the NFL Giants want a parade, let these foreigners parade in front of the oil drums in Moonachie. That's what they should get for moving out of New York!" Mayor Koch was referring to the long-standing tradition of New York sports teams having ticker tape parades on Broadway after winning the Super Bowl, World Series, Stanley Cup, or NBA Championship—and to the fact that the Giants had made a controversial move to a New Jersey stadium in 1976.

It was only January 2, but the Giants' chances were looking pretty good. If they were to win the Super Bowl, it seemed to me that not having a New York City parade would be a terrible loss for the fans, and for the city—as well as for the Giants themselves. For the rest of my drive,

I mulled over possible solutions. I started thinking about the PR opportunities inherent in the situation. As soon as I walked into my office, one member of my team, Malcolm, almost knocked me down in his excitement. "I think we should give the Giants a parade!" he said. At the time, I was senior vice president of Service Establishment Marketing at the American Express Company. It was a great job with enormous responsibility; we handled all the merchants in the United States who accepted the credit card—which meant huge marketing budgets and everything that goes with it.

I told Malcolm that he must have been reading my mind and that I had had the exact same thought on the way into work. I asked him to see if he could reach someone at city hall with whom we could explore the idea of American Express getting involved in making a Giants' parade happen in New York City. I went to my office and started trying to reach someone in the company who could help us design some kind of plan, as well as someone who could approve the idea. Thirty minutes later, Malcolm appeared in my office with a big smile on his face and told me we had a meeting with a deputy mayor in one hour. I, on the other hand, had called six senior executives and been unable to reach any of them. They were all either out of the office or in a meeting. I had never imagined that the mayor's office would want to meet with us so quickly.

Malcolm and I knew absolutely nothing about parades, and yet we did not want to miss out on what seemed like such a great opportunity. So we went to meet with the deputy mayor, who thought an Amex sponsorship was a great idea. He wanted to know how much we would pay, how it would work, etc. Making it up on the fly, I told him we would pay up to $700,000—but only if the Giants won the championship. They still had to win two successive playoff games in order to make it to the Super Bowl, so there was of course a chance there would never even be a parade (which would mean our cost would be nothing, but we would still get some exposure. A win-win.) The deputy mayor asked us to wait and left the room. When he came back, he said he was taking us to meet the mayor. Ten minutes later, I found myself in the media briefing room of city hall where Mayor Koch was just about to give his weekly press conference in front of 150 reporters. I was introduced to Koch, who said hello and shook my hand. A minute later he announced to the press that American Express was going to give the Giants a Super Bowl parade.

By the time I got back to my office, every radio and TV news channel in the city had trucks parked outside our building, and reporters were queuing up waiting to interview me. The story appeared on the front page of the *New York Post's* evening edition and made the local evening news on every network and all the daily newspapers the next day. Over the next week, almost every media outlet picked it up. Although this was long before the existence of social media, the item went viral.

I received many calls from my colleagues telling me what a coup this was. Our advertising agency calculated that we received over $40 million in media impressions over that initial weekend. For me personally, that weekend was very exciting; the Giants beat the San Francisco 49ers (49–3) and got one step closer to the Super Bowl, and a parade.

On Monday morning, I was called to meet with the CEO, who was not happy at all. He wanted to know who had approved the idea of American Express sponsoring a parade. I explained that no one had been available, but that I thought time was of the essence. He told me that one of our bankers was very upset because he was in the middle of arranging a public financing with a New Jersey municipality and believed this "parade business" could cost us the deal. By the end of this meeting, I felt I had been taken to the proverbial woodshed, and the exhilaration I had experienced over the weekend was totally gone. Instead, I was deflated.

On January 11, the Giants beat the Washington Redskins 17–0 in the NFC Championship game, and the Giants were on their way to the Super Bowl to play the Denver Broncos—providing more valuable coverage for American Express about the upcoming parade. The governor of Colorado called and asked me if we would give *them* a parade if they won, and of course I said yes (now that I was a parade expert).

The Giants won the Super Bowl on January 25, 1987, and it was a great game. I called the owners of the Giants to congratulate them and to discuss how the parade should work. However, they decided they did not want a New York parade after all. (The football team and the city were like two friends still bitter over an old fight.) So in the end, American Express received tremendous media coverage for several weeks—*at zero cost.*

Even at that time I knew that something about this situation was very wrong. In spite of not being able to get authorization from anyone, we had decided to seize the moment—and because we took that initiative, Amex got great visibility at little or no cost. But instead of being praised, I had been reprimanded. In fact, I thought there was a very real possibility that I might be fired.

What I realized from this experience was that, because of the way most organizations are run, the potential rewards to a person for taking a risk—rewards that are usually unknowable at the time and almost always end up being relatively minor—are greatly overshadowed by the potential consequences of being wrong. In other words, the fear of losing supersedes the desire to try to win. Most executives and employees understand this equation all too well and act accordingly. I have continually observed this behavior during my thirty-five years of leading and advising companies. I have come to think of this phenomenon as the "playing not to lose" mindset—you don't aim for the win; you only make sure you don't lose. You don't reach for the brass ring; you just make sure you don't fall off your horse.

This psychological aversion to being fully engaged is insidious, almost like a disease. It thwarts innovation and progress. It is a system that almost everyone in an organization follows—unintentionally. No one set it up; it just seems to happen. And even though everyone in the organization realizes that this is the MO, no one does anything about changing it.

Paycheck Maintenance: The "Just Enough" Syndrome

Some years ago there was a senior vice president who worked for me named Mark, who had held the same job for at least twelve years. Although he was ostensibly in charge of "special projects," no one was quite sure what he did. He was known throughout the company as the fixer. He could arrange for a client's son to get an internship, or get four tickets to the World Series. He was always the

life of the party at customer events. Everyone liked him—
bosses, coworkers, and clients alike. One day I asked him,
"So what exactly do you do?" Mark said, without hesita-
tion, "I keep my head down, don't make any waves, and
make sure whatever anyone asks me to do I get done—no
more, no less. It's PCM."

Somewhat taken aback I said, "PCM? What's that?"

"Paycheck maintenance," Mark responded with a sly
smile. "I can't afford to get fired, so I need to make sure I
make everyone happy and, most importantly, that I don't
piss off anyone." He was entirely focused on maintaining
the status quo. He was very deliberately doing just enough
but no more. And Mark did not even hesitate in being
honest with me about it, in part because the company had
always been okay with this attitude. It was almost a given.

Not everyone has Mark's self-awareness, but I am convinced many (if not most) people working in large organizations are functioning by PCM—whether it is consciously
or unconsciously. The problem is, this mindset does not
lead to success or happiness. Whenever I witness this "just
enough" syndrome in action, I imagine a person chopping
wood. Every day, a new stack of trees is delivered. The person wakes up, has breakfast, goes over to the pile of trees,
selects one, and chops it into firewood. By the end of the
day, all the trees have been cut and placed into neat piles
of firewood—after which he goes home, has dinner, and
goes to sleep. The next day he gets up and does the same
thing all over again. That's how many employees feel, that
they're just endlessly chopping wood. Even if you are a vice
president you can feel as though you're chopping wood.
You do the same thing every day; the processes and meetings are relentless and repetitive. And very little happens.

Of course, the just enough syndrome exists everywhere, not just in business. People in politics, teachers, even scientists can suffer from it—putting in just enough hours and enough effort to get by, to do a good job but not a great one. The truth is that most of us have been guilty of this mindset at some point in our lives, but there are varying degrees of the just enough syndrome, existing along a wide spectrum.

At one end of the spectrum there are people who play competitive sports. One of my favorite times of the year is March Madness—when all the college basketball teams in the country compete to determine which teams will enter the national championship. It takes place over three weeks and culminates in the final round to select the "Final Four." The rules are clear: if you win, you move to the next round; if you lose, you go home. These kids play their hearts out. They have one focus: moving closer to the final four. It's tremendously exciting to watch the teamwork, hustle, communications, tenacity, and—most important, the will to win—in action. You see players, coaches, and assistants at their very best. Most of these games are being determined in the last two minutes of the game; the lead keeps changing—sometimes up until the last ten seconds. The players can't afford to even remotely "play it safe." And when a team wins, they have to face another team that is playing just as hard. People in start-up companies operate in a similar way; they have nothing to rest on if they don't win. You can't sort of launch a successful Internet company just as you can't try to score just enough. You have to go all in.

At the opposite end of the spectrum are people who work in civil service agencies. Employees pass a civil service test and get slotted into a specific job with a specific pay grade. Let's say you work in a post office at the counter. Day in, day out, everything is always the same. Employees and their managers come in every day, carry out the same rote tasks, take breaks, have lunch, and go home. Nothing changes. It's very hard to get promoted and virtually impossible to be fired. (So playing not to lose is a very easy game.) But it's not a lot of fun and, most important, there is little to look forward to. Nothing really goes wrong, but nothing really goes right either. It just goes.

Most people fall somewhere in the middle of this spectrum; still, the just enough syndrome is rampant in most big companies. When I interviewed Craig Dinsell, the former EVP and chief human resources officer of the investment firm OppenheimerFunds for this book, I asked if he could explain what causes people to operate like this and whether it was more common with people at the most junior levels of the company, who may behave that way because feel they have no power.

"Actually, this is not a syndrome that occurs only at the bottom," Dinsell said. "It's deep in the psyche of people at the top. The more senior people become, the more they feel that life is narrowing. They can become afraid to experiment, afraid to let go. People need to feel they are in control. Any kind of innovation means moving out of the comfort zone, it's the unknown—whether it's a general manager who has gotten into a particular rhythm or routine (for instance, a person who gets in every day at 5 a.m., etc.) or whether it's someone working in a financial service company who senses that a move out of their established groove may cause them to be vulnerable."[1]

Dinsell told me about a man he knew who was the

chief operating officer (reporting to the CEO) of a large private company involved in distribution and servicing of complex telecom products. This man had been in the same job for many years, and he was liked and respected by all his peers. But he had moved into maintenance mode, rather than taking things forward and being proactive and creative. This eventually led the organization into significant trouble because everyone would talk about innovation and change, but the team lacked the ability to execute because the person who was supposed to be doing it, to be leading them, was incapable of it.

"Was everyone around him aware of this?" I asked Dinsell.

"Yes, everyone knew it, everyone was in collusion. They gave lip service to the need for change, but everyone was in maintenance mode, following suit. This went on until the company hit the wall. Then all hell broke loose."

"What happened?"

"There were major performance problems in the end, and the guy got taken out. Along with the whole team. It was a total shakeup and reorganization."[2] In this case, by playing not to lose, the entire team lost everything—exactly the opposite of what they were trying to achieve.

The real problem with doing just enough is that it doesn't work. People believe that if they keep their heads down, nothing will change. But this is a kind of hiding in plain sight, and most of the time those who are playing not to lose ultimately get fired. In other words, they lose anyway. The thing that they are trying to protect eventually blows up. And yet, the human tendency is to hold tighter and tighter to the status quo even though it's really the antisecurity blanket! To add to the problem, most leaders of large companies are fifty years old and older and are thinking about making it safely to retirement, to ensure that their lifestyle can continue for several decades to come. This clouds their decision-making process in a way that has a negative impact on the organization.

The just enough syndrome is ultimately contagious. If leaders have it, it will in turn shape the behaviors of those who report to them. While no one admits to being ruled by this "getting by" strategy, it is revealed in the nature of their decisions and other actions and is readily apparent to all levels of management (who may have similar inclinations) as well as the rest of the employees throughout the organization.

Employees are affected by this behavior in both direct and indirect ways. Without being specifically told not to rock the boat, the actions, decisions, and communications from their leaders clearly indicate that they should not be bold and seek out newer, better ways to do things. They are not encouraged to call out problems, because then leaders will have to acknowledge them and make tough decisions to fix them. (Remember the snowblowers in Miami?) I am completely convinced from what I have seen throughout my career that employees at all levels would like to do a good job. They may have great ideas to fix problems or to create solutions for customers, but they're never asked. They have their heads down, just trying to get through the day.

To make things worse, often the value statements put forth by the heads of the company are at complete odds with what is really going on. The slogan "Excellence Always" may be engraved on the wall of the lobby, but nobody follows it. And because everyone sees the hypocrisy, it actually backfires. People who look at that statement see that no one higher up believes in it, and the just enough syndrome intensifies.

"What do you think is at the heart of this syndrome?" I asked Dinsell. "I mean, how can a leader who is capable and smart, who sees issues coming down the pike, who reads the *Wall Street Journal*, who knows things are happening . . . Why do they just sit back? And keep expecting everything is just going to go along okay?"

"There are three different things," Dinsell said. "What people believe at their core, what their behavior is, and then what they say. They should all be aligned, but quite often they are not. And men especially—more than women—have the ability to delude themselves. They don't necessarily equate what they do in their career with who they are. In other words, they could be in paycheck maintenance mode, but be thinking at the same time, This is not really who I am. I'm really this other person who is going to do this great thing. They don't want to admit what's actually going on. Because if they did, they may have to confront a whole lot of things they don't want to.

"Of course," Dinsell added, "when there is a major crisis, people are usually shaken out of their complacency. Like when 9/11 happened in New York, or the crash in 2008. Everyone snapped into action. If you don't have a crisis, you can sometimes manufacture one to get everyone motivated. Everyone hustles and does a great job. But when the crisis is over, everyone goes back to regular speed. An organization can't really stay at the kind of high-octane level it takes to negate the just enough syndrome."[3]

I have seen this emergency mode in action many times in companies. It's amazing what people can accomplish when their feet are held to the fire. But then everyone goes back to business as usual, back to PCM—doing just enough to get by. This is a difficult dysfunction to cure, but there are some things that can be done to counteract it.

When I was a freshman in college, I trained to be a lifeguard for a summer job. It was grueling, swimming dozens of laps every day, learning how to rescue people who were drowning, administering first aid, etc. Our instructor was the swim team coach, Mr. McLintock. Coach McLintock was a tough man, and he thought he needed to toughen us up. So after three hours of training and swimming lots of laps, he had us tread water for thirty minutes. During the last five minutes I really thought I was going to drown until finally he blew the whistle. Then he said something I've never forgotten: "Remember: You can't tread water indefinitely; you either swim to shore or you drown."

Many leaders out there are in essence treading water, and if you believe Coach McLintock, such a course of inaction will not end well. Doing just enough is, in fact, never enough.

Dealing with this issue, unlike many others covered in the book, requires a highly personalized approach. Leaders who have gotten to this kind of emotional/psychological place have accumulated negative experiences over the course of many years, which in the aggregate have led them to essentially give up. You can't fix everyone who has this condition, but when I see a leader that I think may still have potential, I make a concerted effort to work with that person.

What works best for me is to begin the conversation with the Coach McLintock story—to get them to understand that treading water is not a solution. Normally they will get that. Next is to find the one or two things they can do differently and successfully in order to help them to reengage. It's all about finding the spark to ignite them again, to create a new path to inspire them to perform to their true potential. Often, they will open up and talk about how they think their "syndrome" developed, and how—now that they are operating at a better level—they are more aware of its origins. This is not psychological counseling; it is real engagement on a one-to-one basis. This does, however, require a time commitment. I need to check in regularly and make sure they remain engaged and are following through.

While I never kept score over the years, I would estimate that about half the leaders I've worked with have reengaged to some extent, regarding their approach to work; the other half never really accepted this challenge and gave up. People who have gradually fallen into the playing not to lose mindset present one of the biggest challenges a leader can face. But if you are dedicated to the Five Principles of Engagement, seeing leaders improve and get closer to realizing their potential can be infectious. I have experienced great satisfaction witnessing PCM leaders improving—as have those who were in contact with them.

I think it is virtually impossible to have long-term PCM employees at companies like Backroads. While of course people who think and act that way live in every organization, Tom Hale's leadership style and the way he embodies his own principles will root them out quickly. Remember that his most important KPI is the trip leader evaluations by customers—evaluations that are intensely scrutinized by his leadership team and him. How many negative reviews will they need to see regarding an individual leader before they take action?

As basketball Hall of Famer Coach Dean Smith once said, "There is a point in every contest when sitting on the sidelines is not an option."

CHAPTER TEN

ENGAGEMENT IN ACTION

"One of the things I learned when I was negotiating
was that until I changed myself I could not change others."

—Nelson Mandela

By now you should be well versed in the Five Principles and hopefully excited about what they might do for you. Whenever I tell the snowblower story in large groups or to individuals in a meeting, I always get the same two reactions. First, they laugh and find the absurdity of the situation very funny. But then I can see the wheels turning in their head, as they recall similar situations they have experienced. What follows invariably is that someone will say, "Let me tell you my snowblower story." Most of these stories are equally ridiculous—and totally true. And all of them could have been solved if people had only been engaged.

The Snowblower Fix

So why were there snowblowers in that Miami store? How they got there the first time is pretty understandable—every store received an allotment from inventory based on some formula. But the story is actually more complicated than that. The fact that this practice has persisted over the years raises many questions and indicates there was obviously a systemic breakdown that occurred over a long period of time. Let's use the Five Principles of Engagement so see how you can identify and fix this type of situation in your business.

FRESH EYES

I saw the snowblowers and, while I'm sure I was not the only one who thought this was crazy, I called it out at our leadership meeting the very next day. Following the nervous laughter and very brief discussion, we moved on to the next subject, the meeting ended, and the issue never resurfaced. If we had been using the new meetings model, the Meeting Czar would have scheduled this item for a follow-up meeting with the right personnel. The meeting agenda would have specified what types of analysis needed to be prepared and distributed in advance. The meeting would have enabled everyone to understand how and why this inventory category was organized and would offer specific recommendations as to how to better balance inventory levels with needs and customer demand by geographical area. I would imagine that, following the meeting, several systemic failures in inventory allocation would have been identified (e.g., beach umbrellas in Alaska), leading to another series of discussions as to what other inventory categories and items might be similarly misplaced. All of this would culminate in a more customer-centric store product mix, where pool equipment would be in Miami and snowblowers would be in North Dakota.

CONNECTING

There were at least two breakdowns in the system that you can address. When Peter's manager and store manager called "headquarters" to plead with them to stop sending snowblowers, who was listening? Where were the leaders of the product line, inventory management, and shipping departments who continued to send snowblowers year after year? A leader meeting with those managers could have picked up this problem.

The second part of connecting involves how many leaders and what level leaders visit the stores. How often do they go? What do they do when they get there? What follow-up occurs after these visits? This is not an "I can check the box because I visited the store last week" issue. You need to visit with intentionality—with enthusiasm. How many leaders actually met Peter, the salesman on the floor in the garden center, or his supervisors? You really want to see for yourself what's going on—give praise to the staff for what you see that's working well, and seek to understand from them what's not. Getting their suggestions about how to fix these problems is essential. You can report back to your team about what you've learned and offer your recommendations about what needs to be changed.

While you're in the store, or the service center, or the waiting room of the hospital, you can talk to customers and find out what they think about the company, the products, your level of service—and they will tell you more than you could ever imagine. Ask the customers why they think a snowblower is on the floor in Miami, and I assure you that you will get some crazy responses. Think about how your business could grow if you reach out to customers, hear what they say, actually listen to it, and then act upon it. It is amazing what can happen!

HOT BUTTONS

Focus is critical. You cannot lead a group by giving them twenty-two items to focus on; yet, over time many organizations do just that. Identifying key hot buttons allows everyone in the organization to focus on the two or three items that will really affect business performance. In this case, there could have been a hot button for returned inventory by SKU (stock keeping unit) as a percentage of shipped inventory. That report would have had red flags every year showing that in certain cities, the number of snowblowers shipped and returned was exactly the same! That would telegraph the problem widely within the organization. It would also have identified dozens or even hundreds of products where similar mismatches exist. Focusing on that hot button would allow product leaders and store managers to realign targets to reflect the nuances of local markets. Keep them simple, stay with it, and watch your organization move in a way you never imagined.

TRANSPARENCY

Your people need information that is timely, accurate, and relevant. And this information needs to be acted upon. Somewhere within the company, there were reports every year that showed four snowblowers on the sales floor in Miami, but did anyone really look at it, or care? There were probably reports that showed items being sent back to the warehouse, every year as well, but was anyone looking at those? Where were the senior leaders who should have been looking at these reports? Every effort needs to be made to allow everyone to have the information they need to do a good job, and then their leaders need to hold people responsible for making sure that the business is moving as desired.

SPEED

Last, but certainly not least is speed. This problem, if the people at Sears had been using the Five Principles, should not have gone beyond two years. Thirty years or more is way too long to have snowblowers sitting on the sales floor in Miami. Large organizations really need to steal the playbook from start-ups and push their organizations to move faster. Months, quarters, and years need to be replaced with hours, days, and weeks. The competitive set increases daily. Every single sector is under attack with online entrants, and you need to run as fast as they do.

* * *

By the way, I did call the Sears stores in Florida while I was writing this book, and I am happy to report that they no longer have any snowblowers on the sales floor.

The Five Principles as a Way of Life

It should be clear by now that these Five Principles are highly interconnected and have substantial overlap. Addressing one principle will invariably force you to consider some of the others. It is not as though implementing any one of these principles will fix the problem, any more than buying a new driver will make you a scratch golfer. The principles are cues—things you can easily focus on every day to make sure you are getting better at engaging.

Many leaders prefer to focus on strategy, new products, new markets, and everything else new. John Wilton from Berkeley told me, "There is an old Irish saying: 'If you don't know where you are going, you are going to end up somewhere else.'"[1] And of course, you do need to have a plan. But while strategy is vitally important, it's the follow-up and the execution that are really critical. In the final analysis, it all boils down to execution. What I have found is that the best and most successful companies know how to execute really well. They communicate, motivate, engage, and just do it.

The Five Principles of Engagement is my approach to improving performance in all types of situations—business, personal, and others. It's a way of organizing your own personal leadership model and provides you with a framework and some tools to communicate and engage with your leaders, and indeed your entire organization. Many of today's enlightened leaders are talking more and more about the need for transparency, speed, and getting closer to employees and customers. But like many things, it's a lot easier to talk about these concepts than it is to actually use them. It's hard work. It takes courage to make tough decisions, buck the trend, deal with very thorny issues, go against the grain, etc. It may represent a substantial departure from how you currently lead and operate, and your inclination might be to be tentative.

It's important that you think and act like an owner. You're Eli Zabar, impatient to wait on any line and you will not allow your customers to wait. You're Tom Hale, and the most important metric you worry about is how well your leaders manage a trip, which encompasses the entire customer experience. You're Don Gogel, and you look at every new deal with fresh eyes and imagine the opportunities with a new company you might acquire. And so on. This is where and how breakthroughs happen.

To begin engaging this way, you have to remember you are a person first and a leader second. This has to be your starting point, your foundation; this attitude just by itself will begin to build engagement. Treating people like people and valuing them and their contributions are fundamental to successful engagement.

It takes a sustained effort to change the set of behaviors that is probably embedded within your organization. Committing to working on the Five Principles is not a checklist you can complete. It's more like a fitness program and healthy eating plan—a way of life you have to commit to. If you only do it once, it's a waste of time, so don't even start. Even if you work at this for two months and then stop, everything will just slide back. Trust me, I know.

Finally, and perhaps most important, I promise you that you will enjoy this process and will reap great satisfaction and rewards, both personal and professional—and that once you begin, you will never turn back. The truth is, it's an engaged life, not just an engaged workplace, that will be your ultimate outcome when you embrace the Five Principles.

The Ideal: What to Shoot For

This last story is a perfect coda to this book. It's about an enormously successful company that has clear values that are fully delivered to their customers as intended. Costco is a company formed in 1983 and in 2015 ranked number 18 on the Fortune 500 list with a market capitalization of over $71 billion at the end of fiscal year 2015.[2] The copy that follows (in the box) comes directly from Costco's website. They define their business model very clearly. What is fascinating to me is the degree to which their leaders execute against their customer mission, as you will see from this story.

On the Sunday before Thanksgiving, my wife and I went to Costco to buy all the items needed for hosting our family dinner for this holiday. The parking structure on 116th Street and FDR Drive in Upper Manhattan was packed, so we knew we were in for crowds and long lines. We found everything we needed and while the checkout lines were very long, there was staff at the end of the lines cheerfully directing customers where to go. We were sent to cashier #15, and I was ready to unload our cart onto the conveyor belt, when suddenly a man named Larry appeared and said, "Let me do that for you, sir."

Surprised, I asked, "Is this new? I have always put my own things on the belt."

He said, "Not sure if it's new, but we need to make sure we keep the lines moving because we are so busy today, and my job is to help get you out of here quickly."

As I turned around, the cashier named Cheryl, who flashed a beautiful smile, said to me, "And how are you on this fine day? I see you're buying up what you need for the holidays."

WHAT IS COSTCO?

We are a membership warehouse club, dedicated to bringing our members the best possible prices on quality, brand-name merchandise. With hundreds of locations worldwide, Costco provides a wide selection of merchandise, plus the convenience of specialty departments and exclusive member services, all designed to make your shopping experience a pleasurable one.

Our operating philosophy has remained simple: Keep costs down and pass the savings on to our members. Our large membership base and tremendous buying power, combined with our never-ending quest for efficiency, result in the lowest possible prices for our members. For additional information, request a Costco Story and/or a My Costco Services guide when you visit any Costco membership counter.

SHOP CONFIDENTLY

We are committed to offering the best value to our members, with a risk-free 100% satisfaction guarantee on both your membership and merchandise. If you have questions about your membership or products you've purchased at Costco, please visit the membership counter at your local Costco or contact our Member Service Center. For more information read our return policy and Member Privileges & Conditions.

WE VALUE OUR MEMBERS

You'll appreciate the quality and value of the products you find at Costco. That's our promise to you. If we fail to deliver on that promise, we'll refund your money. It's that simple.

Source: Costco, "Why Become a Member?"
http://www.costco.com/membership-information.html.

"Yes, we are, thanks," I said.

She then continued, "I know you guys are so busy, and I want to get you in and out of here quickly, and that's what I'm going to do right now. I was talking to my coworker this morning, and we know how much we need to do to get ready for Thanksgiving for our families, so we are wanting to do for you what we would like done for us."

I asked her how long she had worked at Costco and what she thought of the place. Without missing a beat, she said, "I've been here five years, and I love this company. They gave me a good job, it pays well, I have benefits, I get stock, I like my coworkers, and the managers really care about us."

I asked, "How do they care about you?"

She said, "They know we all have families and obligations, and they give us some room to be flexible, you know what I mean? If I have to take my kid to the doctor, they're great with giving me an afternoon off. Lots of my friends hate their jobs, but they need the money so they suck it up."

All this time she had been ringing me up at lightning speed. "I know we are going to get slammed today with volume," she continued, "but I know they hired extra staff and everyone is helping each other out to take care of our members." After she gave me back my credit card, she said, "I wish you and your family a safe and peaceful holiday" and went on to greet the next customer in line.

As we were leaving the store, I looked at my wife and said to her, "That's what it looks like when you get it right."

Engagement is what makes all the difference.

NOTES

Chapter 1: Fresh Eyes

1. Donald Gogel (chairman and CEO, Clayton Dubilier & Rice), interview by Steven D. Goldstein, July 13, 2015.
2. Gogel interview.
3. Lexmark International, Market Capitalization, http://www.wikinvest.com/stock/Lexmark_International_(LXK)/Data/Market_Capitalization

Chapter 3: Out of the Mouths of Window Washers

1. "Undercover Boss (U.S. TV series), last modified January 9, 2016, https://en.wikipedia.org/wiki/Undercover_Boss_(U.S._TV_series)
2. Andrew Florance (founder, director, president, and CEO, CoStar Group), interview by Steven D. Goldstein, June 8, 2015.

Chapter 4: The Importance of Focus

1. Tom Hale (founder and CEO, Backroads), interview by Steven D. Goldstein, November 30, 2015.

Chapter 5: Unleashing Your Team

1. "Volkswagen Emissions Scandal," last modified January 13, 2016, https://en.wikipedia.org/wiki/Volkswagen_emissions_scandal
2. Bill Chappell, "11 Million Cars Worldwide Have Emissions 'Defeat Device,' Volkswagen Says," *NPR*, September 22, 2015, http://www.npr.org/sections/thetwo-way/2015/09/22/442457697/11-million-cars-worldwide-have-emissions-problem-volkswagen-says
3. "Volkswagen Emissions Scandal," last modified January 13, 2016, https://en.wikipedia.org/wiki/Volkswagen_emissions_scandal
4. Jack Ewing and Julie Creswell, "Volkswagen, Offering

Amnesty, Asks Workers to Come Forward on Emissions Cheating," *New York Times*, November 12, 2015, http://www.nytimes.com/2015/11/13/business/volkswagen-offering-amnesty-asks-workers-to-come-forward-on-emissions-cheating.html

5. "Volkswagen Emissions Scandal," last modified January 13, 2016, https://en.wikipedia.org/wiki/Volkswagen_emissions_scandal

6. Jack Ewing and Graham Bowley, "The Engineering of Volkswagen's Aggressive Ambition," *New York Times*, December 13, 2015, http://www.nytimes.com/2015/12/14/business/the-engineering-of-volkswagens-aggressive-ambition.html

7. Andrew Florance (founder, director, president, and CEO, CoStar Group), interview by Steven D. Goldstein, June 8, 2015.

8. Claes Landberg (general manager, YOTEL), interview by Steven D. Goldstein, March 6, 2015.

9. Denis Picard (managing director, Alvarez & Marsal), interview by Steven D. Goldstein, April 3, 2015.

10. "How Mark Fields Overcame Doubters to Earn the Job as Ford's Next CEO," *Forbes*, May 1, 2014, http://www.forbes.com/sites/joannmuller/2014/05/01/how-mark-fields-overcame-doubters-to-earn-the-job-as-fords-next-ceo/#2715e4857a0b2a64b422182d

11. Alex Taylor, "Fixing Up Ford," *Fortune*, May 12, 2009, http://archive.fortune.com/2009/05/11/news/companies/mulally_ford.fortune/index.htm

12. Peter Guber, *Tell to Win* (New York: Crown Business, 2011), 18.

Chapter 6: Connecting Where It Counts

1. Corinne Ramey, "A&P's Imprint on New York Region Fades as Stores Close," *Wall Street Journal*, November 19, 2015, http://www.wsj.com/articles/a-ps-imprint-on-new-york-region-fades-as-stores-close-1447985810

2. Rick McVey (founder, chairman, and CEO, MarketAxess Holdings), interview by Steven D. Goldstein, June 4, 2015.

3. Eli Zabar, interview by Steven D. Goldstein, November 20, 2015.

4. Zabar interview.

5. Tom Hale (founder and CEO, Backroads), interview by Steven D. Goldstein, November 30, 2015.

Chapter 7: Do Ask, Do Tell—and Do Share

1. Joe Myers, "Mobile Subscriptions Now Outnumber People in the World," *World Economic Forum*, November 19, 2015, https://agenda.weforum.org/2015/11/mobile-subscriptions-outnumber-people-world/

2. John Wilton (Vice Chancellor for Administration and Finance, UC Berkeley), interview by Steven D. Goldstein, June 11, 2015.

3. Nick Kostov and Suzanne Vranica, "Publicis Groupe Shuffles Management," *Wall Street Journal*, December 2, 2015, http://www.wsj.com/articles/publicis-groupe-shuffles-management-1449090116

4. "Salesforce.com Market Cap: 48.86B for Jan. 13, 2016," YCharts, https://ycharts.com/companies/CRM/market_cap

Chapter 8: Adopting the MO of Start-Ups

1. Rolfe Winkler and Douglass MacMillan, "The Secret Math of Airbnb's $24 Billion Valuation," *Wall Street Journal*, June 17, 2015, http://www.wsj.com/articles/the-secret-math-of-airbnbs-24-billion-valuation-1434568517

2. Douglas MacMillan and Telis Demos, "Uber Valued at More than $50 Billion," *Wall Street Journal*, July 31, 2015, http://www.wsj.com/articles/uber-valued-at-more-than-50-billion-1438367457; Market Watch website, January 7, 2016, for stock prices of Delta Airlines, United Airlines, and American Airlines.

3. Ryan Bushey, "Netflix CEO Confesses He Tried to Sell the Company to Blockbuster . . . But Blockbuster Wasn't Interested," *Business Insider*, January 31, 2014, http://www.businessinsider.com/blockbuster-missed-buying-netflix-2014-1

4. "Netflix Seen Reporting Web Users Grew to 33.1 Million," *NewsMax*, January 22, 2014, http://www.newsmax.com/Sci-Tech/netflix-reporting-web-grown/2014/01/22/id/548377/

5. Netflix, Inc. (NFLX), "Key Statistics," *Yahoo Finance*, https://finance.yahoo.com/q/ks?s=NFLX+Key+Statistics

6. "Netflix," last modified January 13, 2016, https://en.wikipedia.org/wiki/Netflix#cite_note-13

7. Todd Spangler, "Netflix Far Outstrips Rivals on Hours Viewed, Satisfaction: Survey," *Variety*, January 16, 2015, http://variety.com/2015/digital/news/netflix-far-outstrips-rivals-on-hours-viewed-satisfaction-survey-1201407066/

8. Christopher Harress, "The Sad End of Blockbuster Video," *International Business Times*, December 5, 2013, http://www.ibtimes.com/sad-end-blockbuster-video-onetime-5-billion-company-being-liquidated-competition-1496962

9. Alexis Shaw, "'This Is the End' for Blockbuster Video," ABC News, November 12, 2013, http://abcnews.go.com/Business/blockbusters-rental-end/story?id=20863987

10. "Research in Motion 2007 Annual Report," Ontario, Canada, http://us.blackberry.com/content/dam/bbCompany/Desktop/Global/PDF/Investors/Documents/2007/2007rim_ar.pdf

11. Tom Krazit, "The iPhone, One Year Later," *CNET*, June 26, 2008, http://www.cnet.com/news/the-iphone-one-year-later/

12. Kent German, "A Brief History of Android Phones," *CNET*, August 2, 2011, http://www.cnet.com/news/a-brief-history-of-android-phones/

13. Brian Klais, "Research: How Many Apps Are in Each App Store?" *Pure Oxygen*, March 5, 2013, updated September 25, 2014, http://pureoxygenlabs.com/how-many-apps-in-each-app-store/

14. "BlackBerry World," last modified January 2, 2016, https://en.wikipedia.org/wiki/BlackBerry_World#cite_note-18

15. Will Connors, "BlackBerry to Slash Workforce by Up to 40%," *Wall Street Journal*, September 19, 2013, http://www.wsj.com/articles/SB10001424127887323808204579083250005557232

16. "Smartphone OS Market Share, 2015 Q2," IDC, http://www.idc.com/prodserv/smartphone-os-market-share.jsp

17. Tom Hale (founder and CEO, Backroads), interview by Steven D. Goldstein, November 30, 2015.

18. Eli Zabar, interview by Steven D. Goldstein, November 20, 2015.

19. Bloomberg News, "JPMorgan to Partner with OnDeck Capital for Small-Business Loans," *Crain's*, December 1, 2015, http://www.crainsnewyork.com/article/20151201/SMALLBIZ/151209995/jpmorgan-to-partner-with-ondeck-capital-for-small-business-loans

Chapter 9: Why Playing Not to Lose Is Not the Same as Winning
1. Craig Dinsell (partner, Sheep and Wolves Media), interview by Steven D. Goldstein, March 30, 2015.
2. Dinsell interview.
3. Dinsell interview.

Chapter 10: Engagement in Action
1. Wilton interview.
2. "Costco Wholesale Market Cap," YCharts, https://ycharts.com/companies/COST/market_cap

ABOUT THE AUTHOR

Steven D. Goldstein is an advisor to executives and their leadership teams who helps improve companies' performance through renewed engagement and laser-like focus. He has over thirty-five years of experience working as an operating executive at both global Fortune 500 corporations and midsize companies, as well as advising private equity firms with their portfolio companies. His special talent lies in unleashing companies' hidden assets, transforming employee and customer engagement, and accelerating the pace of decision making and change.

Goldstein has held executive positions with leading global brands such as American Express (chairman and CEO of American Express Bank), Sears (president of Sears Credit), and Citigroup, in addition to being involved in several early-stage enterprises. He has served on numerous boards, including American Express Bank, Jafra Cosmetics, Union Bancaire Privée, Pay-O-Matic, and Big Brothers Big Sisters of New York City. He has also been an investor, advisor, and interim CEO for many venture backed e-commerce companies.

Currently, Steve Goldstein is chairman of US Auto Sales and senior advisor to Milestone Partners. He is also an industrial advisor to EQT Partners (a global private equity firm based in Stockholm). Goldstein earned his BA from City College of New York and his MBA from New York University (Stern). He lives in New York City.

To learn more about Steven D. Goldstein, please visit www.stevendgoldstein.com.